SECRET

Sins

Merlin R. Carothers

Secret sins bring heartache
and pain because they are
orchestrated by an ambush expert

ADDITIONAL TITLES BY
MERLIN R. CAROTHERS

Prison to Praise
Power in Praise
Answers to Praise
Praise Works!
Walking and Leaping
Bringing Heaven Into Hell
Victory on Praise Mountain
More Power to You
What's on Your Mind?
Let Me Entertain You
From Fear to Faith
You Can Be Happy Now
Prison to Praise (Video movie)

Published in Escondido, CA
Copyright 2003 by Merlin R. Carothers
Printed in the United States of America
ISBN 0-943026-36-9

Unless otherwise noted, Scriptures taken from the Holy Bible: New International Version, NIV, copyright 1973, 1978, 1984, by International Bible Society. Used by permission of Zondervan Publishing House, The "NIV" and "New International Version" trademarks are registered in the United States Patent and Trademark Office by International Bible Society.

Scripture quotations from the Holy Bible noted: KJV are from the King James Version of the Bible.

TLB are taken from the Living Bible, copyright 1971 by Tyndale House Publisher, Wheaton, IL (used by permission).

Prelude

Do you have immoral thoughts? If so, you have been lured into a carefully devised ambush.

Some books contain information that is "nice to know," while others contain information that is tremendously important to know. This book contains information that is absolutely essential to your spiritual survival. Strategies will be given to *insure* your survival!

Table of Contents

Chapter 1

She Was Beautiful

She was beautiful. Every curve of her body screamed, "Look at me!" My first glance convinced me that I should look just a little longer. The longer I looked the more desirable she appeared.

The lustful thoughts that flashed through my mind caused me to feel guilty, so I forced myself to look away. But then I realized that soon she might be out of sight; I might not get to see her again. I managed another quick glance. Yes, she was even more alluring than I had at first realized. Despite my best efforts, my eyes kept reveling in what they were seeing. I wondered what it would be like to...

Such scenarios as this were repeated many times over the years until, eventually, they became second nature to me. Images of scantily clothed women seized my attention often, and to my dismay, caused my mind to churn with desires that I didn't want anyone to know about.

Was I abnormal? No. Nearly all men experience the overpowering urge to enjoy the entic-

ing arousal that attractive women can produce. Men enjoy these secret thoughts about
women, and the more they enjoy such thoughts
the more addicted to them they become. What
few men realize is that every time they become
sexually stimulated, a change takes place
within them. Each occasion creates a desire for
yet more stimulation. Eventually the body and
mind crave ever-increasing stimulation. This
change, however, takes place so subtly that
most men don't realize what is happening.

Of course, some men feel no guilt when immoral thoughts flow through their minds; still
they would not want their secret thoughts to
be revealed.

Repeatedly I prayed, "Oh God, please don't
ever let me think such thoughts again!" And I
was sure I wouldn't – and I didn't – until the
next time my eyes beheld an especially beautiful woman. How deliciously enticing she was!
Mmm . . . Then, once again, I determined to
think only good thoughts. But after a while . . .
So many good reasons for me to excuse myself.

After every failure I prayed for forgiveness,
but I wondered if I would ever find a way to not
desire what I, in fact, did desire. I began to fear
that I would never achieve such a challenging
goal. Was there some evil force within me that
was forcing me to think immoral thoughts? Or
was I just a normal man suffering what is a
natural part of man's carnal nature? Why, I

asked, are men forced to wage such a never-ending battle? Why did God permit us to sink into such a dark abyss? Why didn't He make it easier for us to look in the mirror and see a person who is not ashamed of his secret thoughts?

And why did I feel guilty when I read: "Why do you call me, 'Lord, Lord,' and do not do what I say?" (Lu. 6:46).

I knew I was sincerely *trying* to obey Christ; yet I knew I was being disobedient. Second Peter 2:14 (TLB) was written for me: "No woman can escape their sinful stare." This painful dilemma continued for years – even after I became a pastor. I know that other pastors face this same distressing quandary.

When I became ensnared in evil desires, such as enjoying images that have the deliberate purpose of creating immoral thoughts in us, I did not see myself as an active participant in evil. If anything, I saw those persons who created the images as being the evil ones and myself as merely a passive observer. But evil has the power to corrupt anyone who willingly enjoys it, and Jesus told us to beware of anything that provokes evil desires.

It took me many years to acknowledge to myself that my own thoughts were like a bacteria that spreads its influence over everything it touches. Immoral movies, pictures, books and magazines have the power to spread their dominion over anyone who invites their presence. Jesus knew this to be true, and gave us adequate warning. I knew the words He spoke, but I didn't understand them. Or, maybe I didn't *want* to understand them.

Then, one day, God mercifully revealed truths I should have known all those years. Every man who reads the things God revealed to me, will be given the key to be set free from Satan's cleverly devised trap. Every woman, too, needs to know the things that men so desperately need to know. The following pages will expose the ambush that Satan has laid for us.

Chapter 2

Moment of Desperation

I had reached the point of desperation. Despite my best efforts I could find no way to rid my mind of the constant battle against immoral thoughts. Then I heard a whisper:
"Don't look."
That whisper – God's whisper – launched me on a wonderful journey of self-discovery. I began to comprehend what was wrong with me. Gradually I understood that God was instructing me to close my eyes to anything that might cause me to think immoral thoughts. This might *seem* a simple thing to do, but most men know that it can be a nearly impossible undertaking. At first I thought I could *never* accomplish such a daunting task. Maybe, just maybe, I could learn how to close my eyes to immoral pictures, but I saw no way to ever not desire what I in fact did desire.

The next time I saw a seductive-looking woman, I instantly turned away my eyes. Still, something within me screamed, "Look again!" Once again I felt the overwhelming desire to steal just *one more look*. The inner battle that had been raging within me had *not* ended. My lustful cravings continued to exert their almost overpowering influence over me. *But this time I didn't look*!

Then she was gone. I felt like taking a wonderful, deep, cleansing breath. Something else happened within me too. I experienced a strange, pleasant emotion. This feeling lasted only a second, but I was overjoyed. Maybe God *had* changed me, and this wasn't going to be such a challenging endeavor after all! In the months to come I learned much more about that pleasant emotion, and how much I could benefit from it. It slowly dawned on me that Jesus had given us a powerful revelation when He said: "If any of you **really determines** to do God's will, then you will certainly know whether my teaching is from God" (Jn. 7:17 TLB). (bold emphasis added). It took me quite a while, however, to "really determine" to do anything about my problem.

The next time I was tempted to look lustfully upon an attractive woman, I once again quickly averted my eyes. But for some reason, unknown to me at the time, my eyes darted swiftly back to her. My eyes seemed to cling to her as if they were attached to her! "God, what is wrong with me?" I cried. "You told me not to look, yet here I am looking anyway, and enjoying it!" I seemed to be in greater bondage to lustful thoughts now than I had been before. And I felt even guiltier. It was clear to me that I still had much to learn. If you look at women lustfully, you are not alone. Some say that at least 97% of men experience this same problem.

So, with increased anguish, I began crying out to God for some kind of understanding. Step by step, He took me back, way back – back to the beginning of man's first rebellion against Him.

SECRET SINS

Chapter 3

Anyone Who Looks

How long has it been since you heard a sermon or song, attended a Bible study, or read a book about the sin of immoral thoughts? Sadly, few people are interested in learning about this deadly sin. In Matthew 5:28 Jesus said:

"I tell you that anyone who looks at a woman lustfully has already committed adultery with her in his heart."

Did He mean *anyone*?

Jesus then went on to tell us that it would be better for us to pluck out an eye or cut off a hand than to fail to heed His warning!

Such a stern warning should get our attention!

How seriously have you considered Jesus' words in Matthew 5:28?

It is possible that you have read the above verse and felt . . . nothing.

A surgeon can deaden your body so completely that he could amputate your leg and you would feel nothing. I've watched this gruesome procedure during times of war. In the same way, immoral thoughts can so deaden our conscience that eventually we can ignore Christ's warning and feel no guilt whatsoever – absolutely none. Unless we give careful attention to what God says on this subject, we may one day discover that we have made a very costly mistake.

What kind of person does God see when He looks at us? Is what He sees determined by what we *do*, or by the *thoughts* we have?

Many scriptures highlight the importance that God places on our thoughts. To Him, they reveal *the true person we are*.

It is critically important, then, that we pay careful attention to the world of our thoughts: "Our struggle is not against flesh and blood, but against the rulers, against the authorities, against the powers of this dark world and against the spiritual forces of evil in the heavenly realms" (Eph. 6:12).

Understanding *why* we behave as we do, is often an incentive to change that behavior. Our problem is often not "flesh and blood" but spiritual forces that use *whatever works*.

When we understand *why* wrong thoughts are aroused, we have an incentive to change!

These hidden forces manifest themselves when they encourage us to desire anything that God has forbidden. Then, once they gain control over what we *desire*, they are far more capable of controlling what we *do*.

If you have a problem with *any* unhealthy habit, that habit could well be connected to cravings that are generated by those "spiritual forces of evil." They stand against our efforts to rid ourselves of behavior that we know is harmful to others and us.

Satan is waging a frightening war against the human race. His goal is to undermine and eventually destroy our ability to discern God's will. He uses many clever schemes to lure us into thoughts and actions that are designed to destroy us. His favorite and most effective tactic is to convince us that his deceptive temptations are not evil. And his tactics are more successful than most Christians realize. I certainly did not understand for a long time what I was up against.

No Christian would deliberately cause damage to a Christian organization. We might honestly believe that we would *never* do anything to harm our church, but: "Be careful. If you are thinking, "Oh, I would never behave like that" – let this be a warning to you. For you too may fall into sin" (1 Cor. 10:12 TLB). So beware – what you intend *not* to do might be exactly what you end up doing. How might this happen?

First, you could ignore Christ's warning against thinking lustful thoughts. Then you could willingly accept and enjoy the opportunities for immoral thoughts that just "happen" to come your way. The more you did this, *the more you would want to do it*. You could avail yourself of any number of opportunities to enjoy sexually stimulating magazines, movies or live shows. The gradual escalation in the amount of stimuli needed to satisfy your lustful cravings may continue for months, even years. Once you have embarked on that dark pathway, you will follow it until Satan devises a way to utilize you to fulfill *his* plans. **Not one** of us is strong enough to defeat Satan if we are walking hand in hand with him. Every year Christians are forced to abandon their Christian work because Satan lured them down the wrong path – the path to their destruction.

If a young man stores immoral desires in his heart, he may suffer no painful consequences . . . **at the time**.

The young man becomes a successful pastor, evangelist or musician. He looks forward to a promising career, and many people look to him for spiritual guidance. His sincerity and dedication enable him to help many people. But the enemy has laid his plans well. At an unexpected moment, when the most damage can be done, Satan springs his trap and the spiritual leader falls. His followers cry, "How could this possibly happen?" It happened because Satan had devised his trap so cunningly. The young man, and later the mature man, had failed to think about the question Jesus asked in Matthew 9:4: "Why do you entertain evil thoughts in your hearts?"

I have a special concern about the number of pastors, evangelists, musicians and teachers that Satan is leading into the immoral thoughts that may eventually destroy them. They, after all, are many times more effective in their service to God when their minds have been cleansed of immoral thoughts. This is such a serious matter that James tells us: "Not many of you should presume to be teachers, my brothers, because you know that we who teach will be judged more strictly" (Ja. 3:1).

All too often Satan is able to persuade influential Christians of "good" reasons to excuse their immoral thoughts. Of course, they never *expect* to do anything that will bring reproach to the church and other Christians. Such leaders often "drift along" in their sin until something terrible happens to devastate them and their ministries. They permit immoral thoughts to stack up, one upon another. They enjoy looking at things that – one thought at a time – create a hunger for yet more immoral desires. And all the time they sincerely believe that they are spiritually strong enough to keep from doing anything more sinful than "just looking."

Everything *seems* to be going well, and other people have no idea of the evil that is growing in the Christian leader's heart. But these evil forces strive to gain power over us and can actually *encourage* the desire for sexual stimulation. Then suddenly, without warning, Satan provides a perfect opportunity for the Christian to enter into an illicit sexual liaison. There may be no *immediate* negative consequences. It may happen again. And again. But eventually the sky falls in and a promising career comes crashing down.

No matter how charismatic or successful a man may be, if he entertains immoral thoughts he will eventually bring suffering to himself and others.

Lest you think my concern in this matter is unduly excessive, please realize that every year in America many men and women are forced to leave their full-time Christian work because of immoral acts. Their families are thrown into chaos; their children experience confusion, anger, sometimes loss of faith, and often suffer for the rest of their lives. Unbelievers gleefully scoff. God weeps for His children who fail to heed the teachings of His Son. Christ's words make it clear that if a man looks at a woman and indulges in immoral desires, he is committing adultery with her in his heart. He is breaking God's commandment: "Thou shalt not commit adultery" (Ex. 20:14 KJV).

A man who once had a very effective ministry read my book, *What's on Your Mind?*, and said, "Only a very weak-minded man would believe what Carothers says about the mind." In that book I emphasized that we must, and can, control the thoughts that enter our minds. A few weeks after he made this statement, Satan presented him with what he thought was a perfect opportunity to commit a "secret" immoral act. He succumbed to Satan's temptation, was caught, and soon thereafter his ministry came crashing down. I sincerely believe that he never *intended* to do anything immoral; it was his thought-life that set him up for his tragic fall. In recent years other similar tragedies have been widely – and eagerly – disseminated by the news media.

Romans 2:19, 21 (TLB) gives a special, urgent warning to preachers and teachers: "You are so sure of the way to God that you could point it out to a blind man. You think of yourselves as beacon lights, directing men who are lost in darkness to God . . . Yes, you teach others – then why don't you teach yourselves?" A preacher or teacher who warns others against committing adultery is especially vulnerable if he himself practices secret adultery in his own thoughts. And, of course, such a leader suffers severely when others learn about his sin. It is essential that every leader who harbors immoral thoughts pay strict attention to the above verses. For: "What kind of God would he be, to overlook sin? How could he ever condemn anyone?" (Rom. 3:6 TLB). God requires us to have our minds set on what He knows is best for us. He knows that isn't an easy task and that "The sinful **mind** is hostile to God" (Vs 7). Each of us must decide either to submit to God's Word or be hostile to it. The decision is ours.

Many men fail to understand that when they willingly entertain evil thoughts they are being willfully disobedient to God. This then places them at the mercy of Satan's evil plans for them!

All men, young and old alike, need to be fully aware that God seldom punishes us immediately for our disobedience. Be warned, however, that God will not be "silent" forever. In Jeremiah 4:14 He tells us: "Cleanse your hearts **while there is time**. You can yet be saved by casting out your evil thoughts."

Chapter 4

The Beginning

When God created mankind He established His rules of conduct for them. Adam and Eve were required to obey those rules if they wanted to live a happy life. Think of what life on earth would be like today if there were no sin or unhappiness!

God imposed this rule on His new creation: "You must not eat from the tree of the knowledge of good and evil" (Gen 2:17). God did not explain *why* they must not eat from that particular tree; they were simply required to *obey* Him. God doesn't always explain *why* He has forbidden us to enjoy certain pleasures; but He requires that we obey Him whether we understand His rules or not.

And *therein lies our problem.*

When Adam and Eve looked at the forbidden fruit, they liked what they *saw.* They *wanted* it. And no matter how attractive a person may appear, God has warned us that we **must not** think immoral thoughts! We may rebel; we may have all kinds of creative arguments as to why we don't understand such a rule, or why we can't obey it, but we still face the same dangers that Adam and Eve faced. In short, if we disobey God's laws, we will suffer just as certainly as they did. And we will cause others to suffer – just as they did.

We may look at someone who appears especially desirable and hear the same voice that beguiled Eve: "Did God really say, 'You must not eat from any tree in the garden'?" Satan, true to his nature, lied to Eve. God had never uttered those words. Rather, God had told Adam and Eve that they could not eat of just one *specific* tree! Satan, however, is the master of deception. He will whisper to us, "Surely God would not deprive you of the pleasure of merely *looking* at such a beautiful creature." Or, "Surely He will not punish you for doing what is *only natural* for any man to do." In other words, he will use any tactic that he knows will work. Just as Adam and Eve forfeited the blissful lives they could have led in the Garden of Eden, we, too, can forfeit the happiness God intends for us.

Satan did not tempt Adam to sin! Satan avoided a confrontation with Adam and used God's beautiful creation – known as woman – to tempt man. Men still experience the same enticement. We see a beautiful woman and, like Adam, somehow manage to forget what it was that God said we should not do. And, like

Adam, we are quick to blame our failures on the Eves who tempt us.

Obeying God's moral laws may seem to be *extremely* difficult. God knows this, and tells us in His Word: "It is quite true that the way to live a godly life is not an easy matter" (1 Tim. 3:16 TLB). We *must not* ignore God's moral laws simply because they seem too difficult to obey. We can have many excuses that explain why we should be allowed to do what we *want* to do. But if we earnestly seek to please God, we soon understand that: "The wrong desires that come into your life aren't anything new and different. Many others have faced exactly the same problems before you. And no temptation is irresistible. You can trust God to keep the temptation from becoming so strong that you can't stand up against it, for he has promised this and will do what he says. He will show you **how to escape** temptation's power so that you can bear up patiently against it" (1 Cor 10:13 TLB).

If we see an immoral image *and continue looking at it* for even a second, we run the risk of removing ourselves from the protection of God's "how to escape" promise. Once we choose to *keep* looking, we can be tempted beyond what we can bear. Your eyes may have lingered on a provocative image for too long if that image stays in your mind after the visual stimulus has gone. That image is now stored in your memory, and our sinful nature will eventually use it to create even *more* temptation. A vicious cycle of sin has been created. If we really want God to answer our prayers, we must strenuously avoid "wrong desires."

I faced what seemed to be the unsolvable problem. How could I change what I desired? With super-human effort I might be able to change my *actions*, but my *desires?* – no way.

For example, I desire to have a car that runs well enough to get me where I need to go. If I didn't have one, I could survive by getting a bicycle, or maybe even walking. I hope I could keep from grumbling, but it seems *natural* to desire a good car. How could I possibly *not* desire this?

And so the mystery continued – how could I – or any man, change our natural desire to think immoral thoughts? But I knew the matter was important.

For example, how would a man feel if his wife said, "I have always been faithful to you and I plan to continue doing so. But, to be honest with you, I really *desire* to have sex with your friend." That would be like being hit with a sledgehammer! Yes, we know desires are important.

Few, if any, wives have made such a confession to their husbands. But we don't have to tell God what our desires are – He knows the most intimate details of what we want.

Though I have served as a soldier in three

bloody wars, the most desperate battle in which I have ever been engaged is over immoral thoughts. For years I feared that victory would elude me and that Satan's almost irresistible temptations would prevail. The odds, after all, *do* seem to be stacked against men ever winning this vicious battle. Nearly everywhere men go they see women with seductive physical qualities.

Many men do not understand that the same God who created beautiful women also placed restrictions on when and how their beauty could be enjoyed. *They belong to Him!* Any man who fails to understand this will fall prey to Satan's destructive temptations. Once a man really understands that every woman belongs to God, he will find it much easier to cultivate pure thoughts toward her.

God has tied life and happiness into a tightly controlled package that no man can unwrap without His permission. No matter how flagrantly Satan may flaunt his offers of sexual ecstasy to his followers, he can *never* duplicate the happiness that God has offered to those who love and obey Him. I needed to find the motivation to be obedient to Him.

SECRET SINS

Chapter 5

It Isn't Easy

Jesus did not say it would be easy for us to follow Him. In fact He said the opposite. For example, He said: "If anyone would come after me, he must deny himself and take up his cross and follow me" (Mt. 16:24).

Denying self is not easy! Our carnal self craves the gratification that immoral thoughts can provide.

True Christianity is not for those who seek the easy life. Jesus urged everyone to come to Him, especially those who had problems of any kind. But He didn't say, "Sign here, then do whatever you want."

Remember that He told men if they wanted to follow Him they must do something that would be incredibly painful. What is this intensely painful thing that He requires of us? He commanded that we not permit our eyes or minds to participate in any immoral desires. Actually, He was amplifying God's original command in Exodus 20:17: "You shall not covet your neighbor's . . . wife."

Carved in a tablet of stone – by God.

The Bible helps us understand that our eyes are capable of creating lust in our hearts. God created the amazing optic nerves that extend from the eyes to the brain and contain approximately two million fibers! He wants a man to look at a woman and have a desire *for her to know and love Christ!* A disobedient man, however, will rebel and think, *No, I want to enjoy her myself.* Part of me wanted every woman to be pure, but another part of me wanted to use my eyes to enjoy impure thoughts about her. Ultimately, the way a man looks at a woman answers this question: "Do I care more about her body, or more about her relationship with God?"

On the night of His arrest Jesus gave His disciples important advice that they probably spent the rest of their lives wishing they had heeded. Jesus told them to pray that they would not give in to temptation. Then He went a short distance from them and began to pray in a way that demonstrated how strongly we must resist the temptation to disobey God. He prayed so earnestly that His sweat was like drops of blood. He was so determined that He would not give in to temptation that His prayers caused Him intense agony.

Luke heard about this unusual phenomenon and, as a physician, thought it worthy of reporting. It is highly unlikely that Luke had ever heard of a person perspiring blood, but his report is one more proof of the accuracy of the Bible. In recent years medical science has understood and classified Jesus' experience as, "henato hidrosis," i.e., the excretion of bloody sweat under extreme emotional strain. Luke had no way of knowing at the time that many years later his report could be used to once again confirm the Divine inspiration of the Scriptures.

How strenuously have *you* prayed for the strength to resist the temptation to think thoughts that are displeasing to God?

God has given us severe warnings regarding the sin of immoral thoughts. Our prayers for victory over this temptation may need to be more earnest if we are to prevail. When we are *determined* to resist immoral thoughts, our prayers will not be lackadaisical and half-hearted. Once we realize how displeasing to God our immoral thoughts really are, we will pray just as Jesus did, for God's will to be done in us rather than our own.

SECRET SINS

Chapter 6

The Cause

What causes men to be afflicted with the overwhelming passion to think immoral thoughts? Have men always had this consuming desire to look lustfully upon women? I was led to keep focusing on what happened at the very beginning, when God created Adam and Eve.

The temptations we face today are really quite similar to those that faced Adam and Eve: "When the woman saw that the fruit of the tree was good for food and pleasing to the eye . . . she took some and ate it. She also gave some to her husband, who was with her, and he ate it" (Gen 3:6). The Living translation says: "The woman was convinced. How lovely and fresh looking it was!" We men know that our minds can easily convince us that when a woman is so "lovely and fresh looking" that it's only natural for us to desire her.

When Eve looked at and admired the attractive fruit she may not have intended to take that which God had forbidden, but that was

27

precisely what she did. Satan had convinced Eve that God had not treated her and Adam fairly when He had restricted their pleasure. This tactic of Satan has not changed; he still strives to convince us that God's rules are unfair. We will make the same mistake that Eve made if we do not learn to control the focus of our desires. To Eve's mind, taking what God had forbidden seemed to promise more pleasure than she would enjoy if she obeyed God. We, too, can make the same disastrous mistake. We can look at the opposite sex and lust for the pleasure that their bodies seem to offer us.

All the fruit in the garden belonged to God, so He had the right to tell Adam and Eve which ones they could enjoy. Adam and Eve's sin included taking what they knew did not belong to them. Immoral thoughts also involve the desire to take what is not rightfully ours to enjoy.

After Eve disobeyed God, she urged Adam to sin too. That's the way the sin of lust works! When a man lusts for a woman, he wants *her* to be immoral also. He has no desire for her to be pleasing to God – only to himself! And just as Eve encouraged Adam to sin as she had done, women still have the ability to encourage men to sin. Men and women repeatedly fall into Satan's trap of leading one another into wrongdoing.

As I struggled to learn how to think pure thoughts, (and failing many, many times), something became clear to me. Have you considered the significance of Adam and Eve's first reaction after they sinned? Genesis 3:7 says: "The eyes of both of them were opened, and they realized they were naked; so they sewed fig leaves together and made coverings for themselves."

As a result of Adam and Eve's sin, a tragic transformation took place in the human race. Men became obsessed with the physical appearance of women. This obsession may seem natural to us, but it is evidence of our *own* desire to rebel against God. When a man harbors an ever-present desire for a woman's body, he should remember that this is comparable to Adam's disobedience. He should remind himself: "If I do this, like Adam, I would be defying God's will."

Adam and Eve may have wondered what harm could possibly be done if they were to break God's one, seemingly unimportant, commandment. Romans 5:19 says: "For just as through the disobedience of the one man the many were made sinners, so also through the obedience of the one man the many will be made righteous." Adam's sin caused all men to inherit the tragic results of his sin. But Jesus' obedience has made it possible for all men to enjoy the fruit of *His* righteousness. You and I have a choice: We men can lure women into impure desires, or we can encourage them to seek out pure, Godly thoughts. The decision we make in that regard will determine whether we become more like Adam or more like Jesus! And, nearly always, our actions will influence others to follow in our footsteps.

Adam and Eve learned that, eventually, they must face God. They tried to hide from Him, but God spoke to Adam: "Where are you?" (Gen 3:8). Adam answered: "I was afraid because I was naked; so I hid."

Men are now passionately interested in seeing the opposite sex in various stages of undress. But, prior to their sin, Adam probably saw Eve as merely a beautiful part of God's creation; he was *not aware* of her nakedness. He undoubtedly saw Eve in the same way that God saw her. What a marvelous goal for us men! Can *we* possibly learn to see women the same way that God sees them?

For a clearer understanding of this issue, let's now consider God's response to Adam and Eve's realization that they were naked: "The LORD God made garments of skin for Adam and his wife and clothed them" (Gen. 3:21). God *Himself* clothed them! This shows His concern for the proper attire of His children.

Jesus acted in a similar manner. Demons had caused a man to go about with no clothing, but when he came to Jesus his mind was healed, and he sat at Jesus' feet *dressed* and *in his right mind.* Satan's demons whisper, "It is your right to dress in any way you like," but we unsuspecting humans do not realize the source of the thoughts that come to us. When we are in our "right mind," we have a God-instilled desire to cover our bodies in a way that will not create immoral desires in others!

For thousands of years women wore clothing that did not *cause* men to struggle with wrong desires. Even when I was a young boy it was the custom for people to dress in a modest way. When that custom gave way to suggestive and revealing modern attire, a huge amount of suffering was unleashed upon our world as men became increasingly engrossed in women's sensual appearance. As immodesty increased, misery has also increased!

When Adam and Eve disobeyed God, they had no way of knowing the great suffering their sin would inflict upon their children and their children's children. If they had known the pain that would afflict humanity as a direct result of their sin, they surely would have given more careful attention to what God had told them.

You and I have no idea how other people may suffer as a direct result of the decisions we make, but we should give careful thought to this important detail. The decisions we make will most likely help, or hinder, many, many people. Most of us don't like to think about the possibility that our actions may hurt others. Our selfish, fallen nature prefers to focus only on what our decisions may do for *us*. But the Bible exhorts us to think of other people as carefully and lovingly as we think about ourselves. Therefore, we must ask ourselves: Will others be hurt if I follow my desires? Will future generations reap what I sow?

The birth of a child into a loving family can be a joyful event. Unfortunately, however, birth isn't *always* joyful. Many babies are born into situations in which there is no father present to provide a decent life for the child. The man and woman enjoyed themselves, but now the child may suffer. Yes, the man and woman had fun, but another human being will suffer for a lifetime as a result of their few moments of selfish amusement.

It is a fact that thoughts often lead to actions. There is no doubt that immoral thoughts often lead to immoral acts. Jesus said: "It is the thought-life that pollutes" (Mk. 7:20 TLB). And in verse 21: "For from within, out of men's hearts, come evil thoughts of lust . . . adultery, wanting what belongs to others . . . they are what pollute you and make you unfit for God." These words of warning should seize our attention and cause us to do whatever we must in order to make ourselves "fit for God." How can we serve God if we are not fit for His use?

While we are enjoying immoral thoughts, we seldom think about the possible results of them. Instead, we may think *This is only a thought. I don't intend to actually act on my thoughts*. We make this false assumption even when we know that thoughts usually *do* lead to actions.

A man visits a friend, along with several other men, and their host provides cold beer. They pass an enjoyable evening discussing sports and various social and political issues. As the evening progresses they drink more and more beer. Average men enjoying a night out with "the boys." None of them intends to cause himself or anyone else any trouble. But one man, impaired by alcohol, has an accident on the way home and kills someone. The man's blood-alcohol count is above the legal limit. At his trial he pleads, "It was an accident and I'm terribly sorry! I never intended to hurt anyone." But was it an "accident"? No! He drank too much beer, drove his car – and killed someone.

This same principle applies to men who indulge in immoral thoughts. They may never *intend* to do anything that will destroy another's life. They simply enjoy their thoughts, but can easily slip into what naturally follows.

How frequently do immoral thoughts lead to immoral acts? Ask many men what their experience has been, and the honest ones will say, "Yes, if I think about illicit sex I will eventually begin to look for it. And the more intensely I think about it, the sooner I am likely to start looking." This is where pornography plays a major role in the destruction of moral restraints. Those who concentrate on immoral thoughts will eventually engage in acts that hurt others.

A federal study revealed that 80% of serial killers were addicted to pornography when they committed their crimes. This gives us a clue to the source of men's love of pornography. Of course, most men won't become serial killers, but all men who enjoy pornography are fellowshipping with the "Designer of Pornography." Producers of immoral pictures are skilled in making them highly seductive. We have been warned, however, to beware: "Don't you realize that making friends with God's enemies – the evil pleasures of this world – makes you an enemy of God? I say it again, that if your aim is to enjoy the evil pleasure of the unsaved world, you cannot also be a friend of God" (Ja. 4:4 TLB). Could God have expressed more clearly what is on His heart and mind?

The temptation for self-gratification is one of the strongest that humans can ever experience. Of course, we can find many reasons to excuse our indulgence but, eventually, others and we may suffer: "The heart is the most deceitful thing there is and desperately wicked.

No one can really know how bad it is!" (Jer. 17:9 TLB). Ultimately, the only limit to human depravity is the number of creative excuses we can invent. If we *want* to think and act immorally, we can find many "good" reasons to excuse ourselves.

We must reject any effort that this sinful world makes to infect our minds with immoral thoughts. If we don't, we are "making friends with God's enemies" and cooperating in our own destruction.

There will be some readers of this book who believe that they should obey the Bible, yet are still irresistibly drawn toward some form of pornography. If you are among this group, I strongly urge you to acknowledge that *all* forms of immoral images are designed to draw us into what Paul called evil desires (see Col. 3:5).

Christian men, if we have weaknesses in the things we desire, Satan *will* find ways to increase and intensify those desires. Satan is now significantly increasing his efforts to lure Christians into the quicksand of immoral thoughts. If he gains sufficient control over what we think, he can more easily control what we do!

If Satan gains a foothold in our minds, we will not only follow his suggestions. Eventually, we *will not want* to end our pleasure, nor feel any need to do so.

"When you follow your own wrong inclinations, your lives will produce these evil results: **impure thoughts**, eagerness for lustful pleasure . . ." (Gal. 5:19 TLB). It is our *own* wrong inclinations that lure us toward the sin of "impure thoughts." We must strive to resist these inclinations or we will fall prey to an "eagerness for lustful pleasure." Verse 24 speaks of those who permit the Holy Spirit to control their lives, and shows us that changing our wrong inclinations will not be easy: "Those who belong to Christ have nailed their natural evil desires to his cross and crucified them there." Crucifixion is *extremely* painful! God knows that. But unless we accept the deliverance that Jesus offers us, we will continue: "gratifying the cravings of our sinful nature and following its desires and thoughts" (Eph. 2:3). These "cravings of our sinful nature" are powerful and deep-rooted! They demand that we follow our own "desires and thoughts." If you have been satisfying them, you know how strong they can be. Every man needs to understand that: "the lust of his eyes . . . comes not from the Father but from the world" (1 Jn. 2:16). These destructive desires lurk in ambush for us, and, if we satisfy their cravings, they will destroy us at some sudden and unexpected time.

The Bible forewarns us that in the last days men will be especially: "swayed by all kinds of evil desires" (2 Tim. 3:6). Men, God has warned us to beware of the temptations that Satan thrusts at us, but we will not be prepared to resist these temptations if we fail to understand how seriously God takes the misuse of His creation. He created beautiful women, but He also created boundaries to protect them. Ignoring these boundaries is as dangerous for us as it was for Adam and Eve to eat the forbidden fruit!

Never before in history has there been such an avalanche of sexually explicit material flowing into the minds of modern men and women. Most of us are aware that computers connected to the Internet can display explicit images of every conceivable – and inconceivable – act of sexual perversion. (I'm not about to check them out for myself, any more than I would check out a snake to see if it's bite would harm me). Every time a person is exposed to a sexually enticing scene, he either rejects immoral thoughts, and strengthens his moral fiber, or he gives in to his desires and falls into Satan's trap. Heed these words: "Run from anything that gives you the evil thoughts that young men often have" (2 Tim. 2:22 TLB). When we willfully place ourselves in situations where we might think evil thoughts, this opens our hearts to the temptations Satan has devised for us.

There are seemingly no limits to the perversion that has infected the entire world. Sexually explicit programs originating anywhere can be seen in millions of homes via television or the Internet. This should be enough to convince us that we are nearing the time when God's wrath will be poured out upon the disobedient.

I frequently hear from wives and daughters who have discovered that their husbands and fathers are habitual viewers of pornography. These men probably thought that their secret sins would never be known, but then came the advent of computer programs that make it possible for such secret sins to be revealed. Wives are shocked and feel violated when they see the filth that their husbands have been watching. Parents, too, are horrified when they realize what their children have been viewing. Second Timothy 3:1 (TLB) warns us that: "In the last days it is going to be very difficult to be a Christian".

Such days are now upon us, and I fear that many Christians are spiritually asleep. A recent study conducted by a major university reported that each year in the United States, 400,000 children are lured or forced into some form of sexual abuse. Any man who derives such deviant sexual pleasure from this perversion is in danger of severe punishment by our Savior, who spoke of His special, protective love for children.

Ultimately, sexual sin is what *God* says it is,

not what we decide it is! "The Spirit clearly says that in later times some will abandon the faith and follow deceiving spirits and things taught by demons" (1 Tim. 4:1). The tragedy is that: "Many will follow their evil teaching that there is nothing wrong with sexual sin" (2 Pet. 2:2 TLB). Deceiving spirits are constant in their efforts to persuade men and women to disobey God's moral laws. Some of these efforts are so subtle that most people do not recognize what is happening. For example, parents are having difficulty finding school clothing that doesn't reveal increasing portions of their daughter's flesh. Children now are permitted to wear suggestive clothing that draws immediate attention to their bodies – sometimes because parents are afraid to struggle against the anger their children display when they aren't allowed to have their own way. But careless parents ignore the fact that on every street lurk morally sick men whose minds have been infected by the staggering amount of moral pollution that floods the world. Both parents, especially women, urgently need to heed Paul's admonition: "I also want women to dress modestly, with decency and propriety" (1 Tim. 2:9).

SECRET SINS

Chapter 7

My Generation

When I was a boy I never used "bad" words. This may have been a result of the culture of my generation, my parent's training, or the influence of my friends. When I entered the Army at nineteen, I had no intention of changing my way of speaking. One day, however, I salted my speech with a nasty word that caused my companions to laugh. Their amusement gratified me and made me feel important. I liked being the center of attention. The next time I used a crude word it flowed easier from me, though I did feel a pang of guilt.

Gradually I added more crude words to my vocabulary until, eventually, using vile words became second nature to me. My poor choice of words became increasingly vulgar throughout my combat service in World War II. My use of vulgar language came to a climax on one memorable day when a hard-bitten, cursing sergeant said to me, "Carothers, you have the foulest tongue I have ever heard." I suddenly realized that I had allowed myself to become a quite despicable young man. Ashamed, I resolved, then and there, to change the way I spoke.

When I entered the Army I didn't *plan* to do many of the things I ended up doing. I just "drifted" into them. My *intention* was to become a war hero, make my family proud, and – do something important! I never intended to go absent without leave, steal cars or attempt to commit armed robbery. It all just "seemed to happen." I had chosen wrong friends and enjoyed wallowing in feelings of resentment and frustration. I was convinced that the government, the world – everyone – owed me more than they were giving me. Ultimately, my pattern of drifting from bad to worse led me to do things that easily could have ruined my life. Many of those sad details are listed in *Prison to Praise*.

God has declared immorality to be His enemy! As I've already mentioned, I've been a soldier in three bloody wars and saw hundreds of casualties. But all that suffering cannot be compared to the enormous and unending tragedies caused by immorality. No matter how desirable or innocent it may seem to be, immorality can hurt us even more than a bullet wound.

We have the authority and responsibility to obey: "Do not conform any longer to the pattern of this world, but be transformed by the renewing of **your mind**" (Rom. 12:2). Of course, our natural, carnal minds are more comfortable with "this world," but our minds *can* be renewed! We can *learn* to: "Hate what is evil; cling to what is good" (Rom 12:9). "Hate" is a strong word. Once we understand how viciously and eagerly Satan uses immoral desires to devastate mankind, we will find it much easier to hate what our infinitely wise God has expressly forbidden. We are urged to: "Flee from sexual immorality" (1 Cor. 6: 18). We may be tempted to sin at any moment of any day. Ultimately, it is only through standing firm in our commitment to obey God that we will become truly strong in the Lord. Learn to hate what God says is evil!

Being strong in the Lord requires us to have a certain degree of "fear and trembling." There *is* great joy in following Jesus, but reverential fear is a necessary part of being firm in our obedience to Him. Along with our joy, we should sometimes tremble lest we be caught in one of Satan's clearly devised traps.

It is important to understand that when we came to Christ He made it possible for us to be free from our evil desires. Christ's unique method is found in the *truth* that He tells us: "The truth will set you free" (Jn 8:32). I confess that it took me many years to understand that with God's truth we have the ***power to control our desires***! But first we must know *what* that truth is and determine to follow it.

The truth is, temptations come to every person, but *we* decide to either resist or give in to them. Since the temptations offer us pleasure, we face the dilemma of enjoying the pleasures or denying ourselves of them. When we steadfastly deny ourselves, God then causes His Holy Spirit to help us! This, in turn, causes the spirit of obedience to become more powerful within us, so that, when next we are tempted, we are more likely to do what we believe will be pleasing to God.

When our natural sexual desires are not being satisfied, we face a daunting challenge similar to that faced by Jesus in the desert. Jesus, you remember, had been led by the Spirit into the desert to fast for forty days. Satan found Him there and tempted Him ruthlessly. After forty days of fasting, Jesus' strength, both physical and spiritual, must have been sorely depleted. In His weakened condition He could easily have fallen prey to Satan's persistent temptations. But Jesus, as we know, resisted, and defeated, every temptation.

Remember then: When we are deprived of sexual satisfaction, Satan will see our weakness and thrust almost irresistible temptations upon us. He will *press* us to satisfy our desires and willingly help us to think of many self-serving reasons why we *should* do so. "Don't worry," he might whisper. "God understands your needs. Do whatever you need to do."

Chapter 8

Difficult Challenge

When a man becomes a Christian he may naively expect it to be quite easy to follow Jesus and obey His commands. But then he learns that in spite of his faith in Jesus, there are times when he doesn't *want* to obey Him. This is especially true regarding the thoughts we allow to enter our minds. Learning to obey God's laws can be difficult, but it is essential that we *do* learn.

The movie, "Rudy," is based on the true story of a young boy's dreams of attending Notre Dame University and playing on its football team. *Everything* was stacked against Rudy. He had no money, was a marginal scholar, and was too short and too underweight to play football. He was so lacking in physical ability, in fact, that even his intense zeal could not give him the opportunity to play on the team. But Rudy was so determined that he refused to give up. He found a tutor to help him with his schoolwork, studied hard, and refused to stop his efforts to get on the football team. At first

the team members laughed at his feeble efforts, but Rudy, undaunted, ignored their
sneers and kept trying. Eventually the other
players began to admire Rudy's persistence.
Finally, during his senior year at Notre Dame,
the entire team petitioned the coach to let Rudy
join them on the bench for what would be his
last opportunity to play. Seconds before the
season-ending game was over, the team led the
crowd in chanting, "Rudy! Rudy!" until the
coach felt compelled to put this little, underweight young man into the game. At the clos-
ing whistle the team hoisted Rudy to their shoulders and carried him triumphantly. The movie
closed with announcement that Rudy was the
only team member who had ever been carried
off the field on the shoulders of his teammates.

By ourselves, you and I are equally unfit –
unable – to win the spiritual battle against
immoral thoughts. Satan has stacked the odds
against us. Sometimes it seems like the harder
we try to be pure in heart, the more difficult a
challenge it becomes. But Satan can never destroy our determination to trust in Jesus! This
is where Christ can, and will, help us do what
we may not be able to do by ourselves. *Only our
lack of zeal* to win this spiritual battle will be
able to limit us. Jesus touched the eyes of the
men who were blind, and said to them: "According to your faith will it be done to you"
(Mt.9:29). If we have faith to believe Him, He

will touch *our* eyes, cause *us* to see things with a pure heart and actually change our desires! When I understood this, I knew I was on the way to being set free from evil desires!

When the young men of my generation joined the Army to fight in World War II, we fully expected the experience to be exciting and fun. Then we learned that Army life could be extremely difficult. Our rigorous training required us to obey orders that often were difficult – and dangerous – to follow. Tens of thousands of men lost arms, legs, eyes, or were otherwise permanently disfigured. Thousands upon thousands of others lost their lives. The protection of our country, however, required that we obey those orders.

Christian men face an equally difficult situation. Part of our mind says, "I want to obey God, but another part says, "But in *this* situation I *don't* want to obey Him." The desire to look at naked women is a case in point. Part of our Christian thinking says, "I should not look at a woman who displays herself so seductively, but I enjoy it. Maybe it wouldn't hurt too much if I took only a quick look. After all, I didn't cause her to undress."

But Christ came to earth to warn us that when a man looks lustfully at a woman, he has already committed adultery with her in his heart. How long has it been since you heard a sermon or read a book about this topic? If

Christian men rarely hear or read about God's warning against lustful thoughts, it can be easy for them to forget, or ignore, His words.

We should do what the Jews did as they listened to Ezra read God's laws: "All the people began sobbing when they heard the commands of the law" (Neh. 8:9-12 TLB). They were repenting, because they realized they had been disobeying the Lord. Ezra encouraged them, and spoke these familiar words: "The joy of the Lord is your strength." The people then had a time of joyful celebration because they heard and understood God's Words. Once we hear and understand God's Words regarding immoral thoughts, *and obey them*, we too will receive the new joy and strength that we so urgently need.

Later the leaders met with Ezra to go over the law in greater detail. Then people took turns confessing their sins. When we seek God's forgiveness He will forgive, if we have sincerely resolved to obey Him.

In my own struggle to be obedient to God, I grew increasingly aware of verses such as Genesis 4:7: "If you do not do what is right, sin is crouching at your door; it desires to have you, but you must master it." I learned that the word "master" means, "gain control over." The desires for immoral thoughts and actions are "crouching," awaiting their opportunity to gain control over us. But, with God's help, I began to believe that we can "master" or "gain control" over *them*! God spoke the above scripture to Cain, but Cain disregarded the warning, killed his brother Abel, and heard these words from God: "Now you are under a curse . . ." (Vs 11). I knew that if I ignored God's warnings I would also suffer.

We humans sometimes behave somewhat like rodents. Feed poisoned food to a rat and even after it becomes ill it will crave more of the poison – and more and more. Likewise, even after humans suffer the dreadful consequences of immoral activities, they still keep lusting for more and more.

You may never have fully understood God's warnings against the sin of immoral thoughts, but today you can say, "I hear You, God! I'm listening!" We must not be like those about whom Jesus spoke in Mark 4:12 (TLB): "Though they see and hear, they will not understand or turn to God, or be forgiven for their sins."

Since time began, generation after generation disregarded God's will: "The LORD saw how great man's wickedness on the earth had become, and that every inclination of the **thoughts of his heart** was only evil all the time. The LORD was grieved that he had made man on the earth, and his heart was filled with pain" (Gen. 6:5-6).

So God did what His divine nature compelled Him to do. Ponder His actions toward those whose "inclinations and thoughts" were evil. He brought forth a great flood and destroyed them. Some may think that God's actions were too severe, but we do not understand how seriously He takes our inclinations and thoughts.

In spite of man's sins, God did not give up on us. Because Abraham obeyed Him and kept His laws, God promised his son, Isaac, many descendents and great wealth. If we, too, are obedient to God, *our* families and descendants will also benefit. If, however, we do not obey, many following generations may suffer.

At another time God considered the evil behavior of His people and said He was disgusted with them because their *thoughts* and hearts were far away from Him and they refused to accept His laws (see Ps. 95:10 TLB). Sooner or later, God will respond to *everything* we do.

Ponder this frightening reality: If we persist in desiring immorality, God sees it. What are the desires of *your* heart? What would *you do* if Satan were to arrange for you an illicit rendezvous with the most beautiful girl that you have ever seen? Would you remain obedient to God, or would you take the fearsome risk of doing that which He has forbidden? God *already knows* what you would do, because He sees the desires you have nurtured in your heart!

If you have desires that displease God, I urge

you to remember the dreadful punishment He once inflicted on the entire human race. During The Great Flood not one person wanted to die, but only Noah and his family survived. Throughout His Word, God has made it clear to us that immorality is a far more serious matter to Him than we humans realize.

There may be things in our hearts that we ignore because it is convenient for us to do so. But we should never think that ignoring God's anger will cause it to go away. In fact, just the opposite will happen. God will give us time to reconsider our thoughts and actions, and then He will hold us accountable for them. Often God postpones our punishment to give us time to repent. But if we disobey Him we *will* eventually suffer. He has made it very clear to me that he had patiently observed my own immoral thoughts and would have eventually canceled many of the good plans He had for me if I had not changed my thinking. Can you think of occasions when you might have changed your actions or thoughts, if at the time you had a clearer understanding that God might withdraw His blessings from you? God is patient, but He *will punish* us when we continue to disobey Him. We would be wise to avoid God's anger!

Fortunately for us, there *is* something we can do to escape from our sinful nature! God's clear instructions require us to: "Throw off your old evil nature – the old you that was a partner in your evil ways – rotten through and through, full of lust and sham" (Eph. 4:22 TLB). Because of Jesus, we are no longer bound to our old evil nature; we can, we must, throw it off! The reason many Christians have not followed these instructions is that lust is so enjoyable. Jude 4 speaks of: "men, who change the grace of our God into a license for immorality." Be warned, then: If we abuse God's grace and patience by using them as convenient ways to salve our guilt, we are in grave danger.

Women might be more spiritually alert if they realized how frequently men are being drawn into immoral thoughts and conduct. Many wives have said, "I never thought *my* husband would behave as he has." And Christian ladies who dress provocatively would weep with shame if they knew how they cause men to think lustful thoughts. I have spoken to groups in forty-nine states and in many other countries. There I have met with countless men who confess how difficult it is for them to break away from immoral thoughts. *Wanting* to enjoy immoral thoughts is no reason to do so! We dare not risk: "gratifying the cravings of our sinful nature and following its **desires** and **thoughts**" (Eph. 2:3).

Peter cautioned us that with sufficient suffering we will be anxious to do God's will and would not chase after evil desires. He told us that our: "enemy the devil prowls around like a roaring lion looking for someone to devour" (1 Pet. 5:8). Satan *will* devour us unless we learn to control what we allow our eyes to enjoy. The skin of our eyelids is the thinnest on our bodies, yet it wields tremendous power! Too often they are closed when they should be open, and open when they should be closed!

James gives us the wonderful news that if we come near to God, He will come near to us! (see 4:8). This is magnificent news for any Christian who wants to know God better! James also pleads with us to refuse to satisfy our sinful desires. He had learned that such desires war against our soul (see 2:11). We are, indeed, in a war, a war for our very souls. There have been, and will be, many casualties. But if we are obedient to God's commandments, we need not be one of them!

We may think, *I know the Bible.* But we urgently need to hear what it tells us regarding this issue: "Get rid of all moral filth . . . Do not merely listen to the word, and so deceive yourselves. **Do** what it says" (James 1:19, 22). And please don't merely read the words in this book! Do *whatever* is necessary to get rid of what God calls "moral filth."

If Peter were alive today he would still be proclaiming this same powerful message: "he has given us . . . the promise to save us from the **lust** and **rottenness** all around us, and to give us his own character" (2 Pet. 1:4 TLB). Rottenness is, indeed, all around us, but we can choose to have "his own character."

This may seem like a difficult task, but Christ will help us. And: "everyone who really believes this will try to stay pure because Christ is pure" (1 Jn. 3:3 TLB).

One of the most ingenious devices Satan has used to delude Christians is to convince us that since we have received the free gift of eternal life we are now free to ignore God's laws regarding moral thoughts and acts. Consciously or unconsciously some Christians think they can do what they know God has forbidden and not be punished – or at least, not too severely. Jude saw this tragic belief developing in the early church and, alarmed, reminded them that although God had rescued an entire nation of people from slavery in Egypt, He then caused *every one* of them who did not obey Him to die in the desert. Jude also urged them to remember the cities of Sodom and Gomorrah, and how God destroyed them because they had become "full of lust." Jude warns us that in the latter days men would strive to: "enjoy themselves in every evil way imaginable" (Vs 23 TLB).

If you have permitted immoral desires to fester in your heart, they will become increasingly capable of causing you to make wrong decisions. You may experience only an occasional or momentary lustful desire – for now. But take no comfort in that. Our sexual desires lie coiled within us like a tightly compressed spring and, when we entertain an immoral desire the spring is compressed just a little bit more. Every downward pressure on the spring makes it more likely to explode upward. Finally, when enough constant pressure has been exerted on it, it breaks its restraints and bursts forth in all its unconstrained passion. Then, like the fallen Christian leader mentioned earlier, the unwary person finds himself doing things he never intended to do. We may not understand how or why such scenarios occur, but that's why God urges us to do whatever is necessary to prevent ourselves from thinking immoral thoughts. He knows that when immoral thoughts lurk in our hearts we are easy prey for the trap Satan sets for us.

If we should tumble down a steep flight of stairs, we might wish that the law of gravity did not exist. In the same way, when lustful thoughts tempt us we might wish that God's moral laws did not exist. But they do. And when we break those laws, we – and others – will inevitably suffer.

The Holy Spirit wants to change the desires of our heart so that we will actually *desire* to please God! But until that happens, we must battle our minds when they are set on what our sinful nature desires.

The Jews were already aware that God had condemned the *act* of adultery, but Jesus revealed what happens when a man even looks at a woman with a lustful eye. The Bible tells us that – in layman's terms –

Fantasies that would be evil if acted out are – in God's eyes – a part of the act itself!

Yes, a lustful eye does cause a craving for immoral acts! Our eyes are fully capable of convincing us that what we see is what we want. True, a man might look at a thousand women with lust in his heart, and still not carry out the act. But when his sinful desires are indulged frequently enough, and grow strong enough, they *will* take over. Then, no matter how strong his moral values may have been before, he will seek to complete the physical act. His carnal desires have overwhelmed his desire to please God, and have even overcome his fear of displeasing God!

Some men may tell themselves, "It's okay to look as long as I don't touch." But when a man looks lustfully often enough, he will eventually "touch." His reason and Christ-like values fly out the window.

Jesus knew that men's eyes could cause them to think immoral thoughts. This was such a serious matter to Him that He told us emphatically:

"If your eye causes you to sin, gouge it out and throw it away. It is better for you to enter life with one eye than to have two eyes and be thrown into the fire of hell" (Mt. 18:9). Of course, the loss of one eye would not prevent a man from using his remaining eye to do whatever he did with two eyes. Jesus used this extreme example to emphasize how necessary it is for us to make every effort to use our eyes only in ways that will not cause us to be punished by God.

Jesus could not have emphasized more clearly that immoral thoughts should not be taken lightly. Every time a man looks at a woman, he stores up either good or evil in his heart. If we choose to store evil thoughts, they will eventually produce evil results.

Even now, at this very moment, your mind is "stored up" with the thoughts and desires that will influence your future. What you have stored in your mind is far more critical than you may imagine! A camera lens opens; a picture is stored on a film. You place that picture in an album and look at it when you choose to do so.

Every waking hour each of us makes conscious or subconscious decisions about how relevant the Bible is to our daily lives. Many decide that the Bible *is* true and relevant, but also conclude that its standards of conduct are too high. They prefer to pick and choose the standards they will follow and those they will disregard.

This is wrong-headed thinking! No one should think of the Bible as a chain around his neck, but, rather, as a life preserver provided by God to keep us afloat in the storm-tossed seas of life. Those who choose the easy, self-indulgent route will never enjoy the help and blessings that He promises those who earnestly strive to please Him.

My body and spirit have never been ravaged by alcoholism, but I have worked with many who were struggling to recover from this deadly addiction. The first and most vital step toward recovery is for the sufferer to admit that he is an alcoholic. Before he reaches that point, he may say, "I may eventually become an alcoholic," or, "I don't drink enough to hurt myself," or any number of other excuses that don't require the humiliation of saying, "I am an alcoholic."

However, once a man admits to being an alcoholic, he is then ready to embark upon the path to recovery. This is not an easy path to travel, but with time, persistent effort and God's help, he can free himself from his craving for alcohol. The average alcoholic, unfortunately, often refuses to recognize that he must stop drinking. All too often something drastic – even tragic – must happen before he will finally change his behavior.

This same harsh reality is true for those who enjoy adulterous thoughts. "Why," they ask themselves, "should I change what I'm doing when I enjoy doing it? I don't consider myself an adulterer!" But, like the recovering alcoholic, he must inevitably confront the fact of his sin before he is likely to change. If we convince ourselves that nothing drastic will happen as a result of our immoral thought life, we can feel quite comfortable in our sin.

Not many Christians have the courage to say, "I am an adulterer." They would much prefer to say, "I'm not as good a Christian as I would like to be," or, "I wish I could do better," or, "I'm doing the best I can," or any number of excuses. Anything but to clearly and humbly define themselves as active, present tense adulterers.

But Jesus said that any man who looks at a woman lustfully *is* an adulterer. Once we admit our guilt to ourselves, and to God, we are then ready to seek and receive His forgiveness and help. We don't need to live in fear of God if we follow His simple promise: "If we confess our sins, he is faithful and just to forgive us our sins, and to cleanse us from all unrighteousness" (1 Jn. 1:9 KJV).

If Christ Himself should appear and tell us, "Don't ever do that again!" it would be easier for us to never repeat that act again. But since God seems so far away, we may find it difficult to attach proper importance to what He thinks about our thoughts and actions. We might even be praying, "God, please reveal Yourself to me so I will know if what I'm doing is wrong." Then, if He doesn't immediately reveal Himself, we may continue to drift along in our rebellious ways.

God knows not only what we are *doing*, but also what we are *thinking* about doing. We may have displeased Him so often that His very existence has become unreal to us! If so, we must declare war on anything that separates us from Him. As we wage war against our unholy thoughts, we will gradually draw closer to God and gain new insights into what pleases or displeases Him. If you have created a deep chasm between yourself and God, it is critically important that you take immediate action to conduct yourself as you believe Jesus would.

When God commands us to do, or not to do, something, our decision to do the right thing will be easier if we have a clearer understanding of the magnificent wonders He has created. Look at what appears to be a lone star and consider that it may actually be a galaxy composed of billions upon billions of stars! God's creation *is* inconceivably awesome! Then, lift your hand and locate a star that appears to be only a finger's width from the first star. Realize, however, that the distance between the two could actually be trillions of miles! This God, who created the marvels of our incredibly vast universe, is the One before whom we will someday stand to give a full account for *everything* we have done!

SECRET SINS

Chapter 9

The Right Side of the Brain

A book I read about the art of drawing, posed an interesting theory that intrigued me. This theory maintains that after the left side of our brain has mastered the techniques of learning to read, language skills, mathematics, etc., it is then not interested in pursuing the tedious process of learning how to draw. The author suggests that if the *right half* of our brains can be enlisted in this effort, we can then more easily learn to draw.

My first thought was that this was some far-out theory too bizarre to be taken seriously. But I decided to give it a try anyway, to see if there was *anything* I could draw. Until that moment, at age 75, I had never been able to draw anything that looked even remotely realistic.

The author suggested that I begin by trying to draw a picture of my hand. The finished result looked more like an apple with sticks coming out of it. Then I followed other suggested exercises to see what would happen if I could learn to draw using the right side of my brain instead of the left.

To my astonishment my drawing actually looked like a hand! This led me to think about other ways in which the brain may be compartmentalized. When we go to sleep, for example, part of the brain shuts down while another part goes to work. This other part creates dreams that seem actually to take place. Later, when the other part of the brain wakes up, it takes over. No matter how hard we try, the awakened, conscious part of the brain is not able to recreate the clear and realistic pictures we saw in our dreams.

The fact that our brain is compartmentalized, is not an adequate representation of our spiritual conflicts, but it does illustrate the fact that we can have an inner spiritual battle and yet not even know that a conflict is taking place. I remember horrible decisions that I have made while at the time being completely unaware that a spiritual battle was taking place. I did what I wanted to do. I paid little attention to what I knew the Bible says and found some reason to excuse myself – even though some part of my mind had to have known that I was being disobedient. If you should ask me to explain some of my decisions, I would have to give the honest answer, "I don't have an explanation."

Part of us wants to obey God, so we can enjoy

the resulting benefits, but another part of us says, "No, I don't want to obey Him, and I don't believe that He will cause me to suffer for my disobedience." Once I began to understand this spiritual conflict, I began to realize that even though I had received a new life in Christ, there was still a part of me that wanted to rebel. This rebellious part, I now know, will eventually take over if given encouragement. But our disobedient nature can be defeated! With Christ's help, we can learn ways to subject ourselves to God's will, not our own!

In chapter seven of Romans, Paul shared his struggle with his own disobedient nature. A Christian man may not want to look lustfully upon women, but sometimes he may find himself doing so. If he commits this sin frequently enough, he will eventually forget the significance of his actions and, in time, will be unashamed when he disobeys God. Fortunately, the Bible gives us strategies that will enable us to win the battle against our sinful nature. Later on I will list them. Not only *can* we do these things, we *must* do them if we hope to escape the terrible results of disobedience to God.

Some Christian men may need to be subjected to a massive dose of the fear of God! A fear of the Lord, however, *requires* us to examine the results of everything we do. *One sure result of disobeying God is the eventual loss of our happiness*. So many men are unhappy, and do not realize that their immoral thoughts are the **cause** of their unhappiness

Men don't ask to be drafted to fight in a war, but they do get drafted, and they do end up on battlefields. Many of those draftees are wounded and permanently disfigured. Many others die. But there is another war being waged. Many sustain grievous injuries; countless others die. We may not see these casualties, but we hear about them frequently. Reliable data reveal that every year, worldwide, over one million young girls are snatched off the streets of their communities to be sold as sex slaves. These girls do not choose to become prostitutes; they are coerced and brutalized into it. They are locked in closely guarded rooms and beaten or starved until they agree to submit. Their terrified parents have no idea what has happened to their children. These children are feeding the lusts of men who have become slaves to their perverted sexual desires. Children have become casualties in the terrible war being waged by sick and evil men who crave sexual gratification at any cost.

What forces caused these men to sink to such utter depravity? We Christian men must find the answer to this question, and then strive to eradicate this ungodly evil.

You and I must learn to wage war against this wickedness that causes such suffering!

For our prayers to be answered, we mu.. heed Isaiah 59:2: "Your iniquities have separated you from your God; your sins have hidden his face from you, so that he will not hear." Our immoral thoughts may be the very reason why many of our prayers go unanswered. But our loving and merciful Heavenly Father will forgive us if we sincerely repent and turn away from our sins with determination.

Every year immoral thoughts and actions cause millions of people to contract a variety of sexually transmitted diseases. A recent report by the Center for Disease Control (the CDC) in Atlanta, Georgia, estimates that in the U.S. alone there are **sixty-five million** people who suffer from sex-related diseases! And the problem is growing! Each year **millions** more people in our country contract one or more of these diseases. Some of these diseases can lie dormant for years and cause blindness, infertility and death long after they are contracted. And what is now alarming informed people is that according to a report issued by the CDC in 2001, condoms *do not* protect the user from or prevent the spread of some of the more virulent sexually transmitted diseases such as: syphilis, gonorrhea, genital herpes or human papilloma virus. Unfortunately, such reports as these are seldom given adequate coverage in our newspapers, TV news, or in our classrooms.

These troubling facts should warn us that a moral disaster is sweeping across our nation. Tragically, every person who indulges in immoral thoughts thinks, *Sounds terrible, but it will never happen to me.* Even Peter sincerely believed he was being truthful when he assured Jesus that he would *never* forsake Him. Those who think they will never give in to temptation, even while they are actively subjecting themselves to it, need to remember that Peter did exactly what He told Jesus he would never do. Why? Because he failed to heed Jesus' admonition to pray that he would not fall. Therefore, *Strategy #1* is – Ask God to help you change your thoughts and desires. What a huge mistake we men make when we choose to disregard Jesus' words to us!

Ladies, you may already know this, but I'll remind you: An unscrupulous man will tell a woman *anything* in order to have his way with her. That isn't fair, but it is a sad fact of life. Further, either party to an illicit liaison could have a life-threatening sexually transmitted disease and not even know it. Even worse, there are those who will "forget" to mention that they have such a disease. They may not intend to infect their partners but, in the heat of their passion, are overcome by their own selfish interests.

If you deceive your spouse by having sex outside of marriage, you have no dependable reason to expect that your illicit partner will be truthful with you. A woman can tell a man that she is on birth control, when actually she isn't. She can have his baby, support the child for 17 years, then win a lawsuit that requires the father to pay her 18 years back child support. Men, too, will lie and claim that they are not married, when they are. Immorality is nearly always accompanied by deception. Men and women need to be aware that *sexual activity is serious business!* God Himself planned it to be so.

A person cannot become addicted to heroin until heroin has been introduced into his or her body. We could watch someone else take this drug and wonder how he could be so self-destructive. But once we, ourselves, have taken heroin, and our brains have felt its addictive power, we, too, would begin to crave it. The more frequently we enjoyed the drug, the more our body and mind would desire it. In time, no matter how powerful our self-preservation instinct might be, our addiction would cause us to scream for more heroin. Without help of some kind, we would lie, steal, and do anything else in our power to feed our addiction. An addiction to sexually immoral stimulation is very similar to this.

In *Healing Life's Hidden Addictions*, pp 145 ff, Dr. Archibald D. Hart writes, "The most powerful force in the physical world is not the nuclear bomb – but sex! Addictions to alcohol and cocaine may be major problems for our age, but they pale into insignificance when compared with the ravages of sex gone wrong."

In *Temptations Men Face*, pp 54 ff, Tom L. Eisenman writes, "If perverted, sex is a power that destroys. It holds men captive. Turns quickly to obsession. Burns with lust. It demeans human beings, reducing them to things to be used, abused and discarded."

Once a man becomes addicted to the "pleasure" that immoral thoughts can give him, the sexual stimulation that gives him pleasure requires an increasing element of degrading perversion. That is, the more frequently his immoral desires are satisfied, the stronger his desires become. An addicted Christian man might ordinarily find the idea of kidnapping a child for the purpose of sexual satisfaction unthinkable and repugnant, but if he is introduced to a beautiful, young girl who is enslaved in that diabolical system, he might easily give in to the temptation.

Suggestive ideas can come to us in the most unexpected ways. A thought comes to mind – any thought – and we may be unaware of its source. For example: We might think, *I want a cup of coffee*. This thought wasn't the result of our being thirsty, but rather from times when we enjoyed the taste and smell of coffee. So we think, *I want some coffee*. We don't think to ask ourselves, *why* do I want coffee? We simply respond to the thought and look for coffee.

Our minds can easily develop a habitual way of thinking. Our moral choices can become so ingrained and habitual, that ultimately the mind does its own deciding. Most of our "I wants" are not necessarily morally wrong, but our minds can take the immoral "I wants," and pursue actions that can destroy us.

There are evil things that are difficult to hate if we have never suffered from them. For example, if you or someone you love has never been addicted to drugs, it may be quite difficult for you to hate that particular addiction. But addictions usually come slowly and subtly. Then, gradually, the body wants more and more of the substance in order to be satisfied. No one ever intends to become an addict. But they do.

Immoral thoughts work in the same subtle way. First we are gratified by something that is just a little bit risqué. Then we want more of the same. In time the addiction can grow and grow until it reaches the level of the hardened and hopeless heroin addict. At first, neither addiction *seems* to be all that powerful, but gradually it does control the person who chose to embrace it. Countless men have described their addictions and told me, "I was sure *I* would never become addicted."

An eye specialist I consulted explained to me a strange phenomenon that takes place between our eyes and brain. If we have a defective lens in one of our eyes, it can cause our brain to receive distorted images. This condition can persist for many years. What if we were to undergo a lens transplant? Would our brain then receive a clear, undistorted image? Sometimes, yes. This would depend on how long the brain has been receiving distorted images. Often, however, the brain continues to receive indistinct images even after a new lens is implanted. The eyes have, in fact, trained the brain! Sometimes the brain never recovers from its years of receiving distorted images.

As the doctor explained this to me, I realized that this condition is similar to that of many men when they become Christians. If they have been looking at women through distorted, lustful eyes long enough, they may have great difficulty learning to see them through their new godly eyes. This may be why so many Christian men still wrestle with immoral thoughts. But how thankful we can be that, because of Jesus, our old, sinful desires can be changed into new pure desires! No matter how long we may have thought the way Satan wanted us to think, God will help us change if we really want to see women as He sees them! *Strategy #2 –* Ask God to help you see women as He sees them.

Remember how angry Jesus became when He came upon the moneychangers in God's temple? Other people saw no reason for His anger, but Jesus had God's point of view and God's anger stirred in Him. He overturned tables and used a whip to drive the men out. If we could know God's opinion regarding immorality and immoral thoughts, we would find it much easier to heed His commandment to be pure in heart. We can learn to have more of His perspective, but it takes a real desire to become obedient to Him rather than to be satisfied with ourselves as we are.

When God first told human beings that they were forbidden to even **want** another's spouse, I believe Satan launched a massive attack to prevent us from obeying God's commandment not to covet. Satan had been cast from Heaven and his relationship with God destroyed. Now his plot was to lure men and women into rebellion against God so that their relationship with God would also be destroyed.

When Adam and Eve disobeyed God they became – quite unintentionally – partners with Satan in his desperate battle against God. Their lives, and ours, would never again be the same. Strife, struggle and pain would become the new way of life for humanity. But Satan's plot did not end there. He knew that man's carnal desires were an important key in persuading them to disobey God.

God commanded man not to lust after his neighbor's wife. A man may be careful to obey God until his neighbor's wife becomes so appealing to him that he no longer wants to resist her. Then, casting aside his desire to obey God's commandment, he disregards God's will, and eventually he, his neighbor, and others suffer. Disobedience to God does extract a terrible penalty.

Jesus said that if we caused someone to sin, we would be better off if we were thrown into the sea with a rock tied to our neck (see Mt 18:6). What a strong statement! Imagine the terror you would feel if you knew you were about to be drowned in the sea by a rock tied to your neck! But Christ has spoken: If we, by our immoral actions, cause another person to sin – we will eventually suffer terribly!

Adam began this tragic sequence. Although God created Adam to be perfect, he still became infected by sin! Men, if Adam could fall, *we can too*! We must be alert! If Adam's sin caused the fall of the entire human race, can we have any hope that *our* sins will not cause others to become sinful? If a man causes a woman to sin, will he not be responsible for her sin? And if a woman tempts a man to sin, will she not be responsible for his sin?

Encouraging another person to disobey God may be worse than the sin of our own disobedience!

Jesus said all the commandments were

summed up in this one: "Love your neighbor as yourself" (Mt. 22:39). If you believe that immorality will be punished by God, don't cause "your neighbor" to be punished. Jesus said those who encouraged or enticed others to sin, would suffer great "woe." (see Luke 17:1) There will always be those who tempt others to sin, but Jesus warned that He takes this offense *very seriously! Strategy #3* – Don't cause, or want, another person to sin.

If Satan has used us to lure others into sin, we certainly do not want our families and friends to know, but Jesus promised us that one day all misdeeds would be exposed. If you have thoughts that you are ashamed of, you are the person to whom Jesus was speaking!

But even if we understand that our sins can be exposed at any time, we may still believe ourselves incapable of changing. If so, we are the person to whom Jesus was speaking when He said that everyone who sins is a slave to that sin (see Jn. 8:34). *Nothing* forces us to have evil desires except the *choices we make.*

For about the first two hundred years of our nation's history, men and women made a diligent effort to obey God's moral laws. Women were careful to dress modestly in public, and men agreed, by common consensus, that this was God's will. During those years, it was socially unacceptable for a woman even to expose her ankles!

Further, a man was not permitted to kiss his sweetheart until they were engaged. That first kiss signaled their engagement, and engagements in those days were almost never broken. Both the betrothed and society expected the subsequent marriage to endure "until death they did part."

The day came when women began to reveal their ankles – and more. Men did not object, and the rest, as they say, is history.

The sin that infected our world as a result of Adam and Eve's disobedience, has unleashed the terrible strife and chaos that plagues us to this day. In recent years, this moral decay has become so common that it may seem impossible to do anything about it. But there *are* things we can do. We can strive to be one of those who are *not* disobedient to God, and we can stop making excuses such as, "I can't stop what goes on in my mind." Or, "I'm only human." Or, "This is the way God made me." We may devise a thousand excuses for our actions, but God always holds us responsible if we break His law. *Strategy #4* – Stop making excuses for lustful thoughts.

If we do not learn to resist Satan, he will increase his enticements. He will not stop until he has destroyed our ability to serve God. It would be dreadful to miss the opportunity to live our lives in such a way that we are pleasing to the One who gave us His gift of eternal life.

Once we depart this life, our opportunity to serve Him here on earth will be gone *forever*.

If you are married, consider your attitude toward your wife. If another man wants to have sex with her, will you ignore his advances and say, "That's the way men are"? Or will you demand that the man leave your wife alone?

If a man by some surreptitious means obtained a picture of your wife in the nude, would you object if he were to show it to his male friends? Would you accept this violation as "only natural," and shrug, "That's the way God made him?" Or would you become violently angry – because that's the way God made *you*?

It is unacceptable in almost every society for a man to want another man's wife. We *know* it is wrong, but some men devise ways to justify their lust for other men's wives. Men who want to obey God should: "Treat the older women as mothers, and the girls as your sisters, thinking **only pure thoughts** about them" (1 Tim. 5:2 TLB).

Men in every culture have killed other men for making sexual advances toward their daughters. Yet these same men might feel justified in making improper advances toward *other men's daughters*! We may twist our values to fit our own desires, but God doesn't. He judges all men on the same basis. We can almost feel His anger in Jeremiah 5:8: "They are well-fed, lusty stallions, each neighing for another man's wife." Such is the present condition of many men – even Christian men.

Strategy #5 – Think only pure thoughts about any woman.

God sees sexual immorality as a horrible misuse of the creative power He gave us. He intended sex to be *His* instrument for creating a living, spiritual being who will endure forever. God intends for everything connected to sex to be used only within the strict boundaries He established.

Chapter 10

Crucial Lessons From Job

Long before God had given Moses His law, Job wrote:

"I made a covenant with my eyes not to look lustfully at a girl" (Job 31:1). *Strategy #6 –* Make a covenant about what you will look at.

Job instinctively knew God's will even before God had given His law! Every man has that same inner-knowledge. If you have not made that covenant with your eyes, ask yourself why. You know God's will, and you have His Holy Spirit's help. You even have His gift of eternal life. Yet you still have not been as obedient to God as Job was.

Job kept his covenant with his eyes, and it is possible for every Christian – with the help of the Holy Spirit – to make and keep this same covenant! Every time a man sees a sexually appealing woman, he has a wonderful opportunity to follow Job's example. But remember, this opportunity lasts for only a second. Right then – at that instant – he can choose to turn his eyes away or he can choose to indulge his desire to look just a little longer. I understand this temptation well, because I gave in to it thousands of times. Now I realize that I did this because I *enjoyed* doing so.

If we indulge a desire to enjoy something that God has forbidden, we increase the power of that forbidden desire. This makes it *more difficult* to resist such desires the next time. But if we deny a sinful desire, it becomes *easier* to deny it the next time! Job shared great wisdom when he wrote: "Those with pure hearts shall become stronger and stronger" (17:9 TLB). It took me a long time to understand that with God's help we *can* train our minds to think pure thoughts rather than immoral ones. Job's spiritual awareness, and desire to please God, are examples every Christian should follow!

Job revealed what many men have yet to learn: "Lust is a shameful sin" (31:11 TLB). Lust is a covetous desire to take something that does not belong to us. God's will, that we turn away from sin, is not going to change just because we don't understand why immoral desires are such a shameful sin.

Lust is shameful because it is a habit that *we* establish ourselves. Aristotle wrote: "We are what we repeatedly do. Excellence, then, is not an act, but a habit." Horace Mann, the educator, said: "Habits are like a cable. We weave a strand of it everyday." Breaking long established habits can be extremely difficult!

The thoughts that flow through our minds are not a small, insignificant part of our Christian life. Rather, our thoughts are at the very core of the person we are! The moral goals we set for ourselves should reflect the standards we believe Jesus followed.

A Roman Centurion asked Jesus to heal his paralyzed servant. Jesus saw that the Centurion believed in Him, so He said: "It will be done just as you believed it would. And his servant was healed at that very hour" (Mt. 8:13). *Strategy #7* – Believe Jesus can heal your impure thoughts and desires. He will heal our diseased, immoral thoughts when we believe Him. When His disciples were afraid because of a violent storm, Jesus asked them why they had so little faith. We *can* believe that Jesus heals our unclean minds!

When I learned to close my eyes to whatever stirred immoral desires, then God began *His miracle* in me. *My desires* began to change! To experience that miracle is as exciting as it would be to see a man raised from the dead!

SECRET SINS

Chapter 11

Christian Perfection

Just a few generations ago most of the pulpits of America declared the importance of striving for Christian perfection. These days, one who strives for Christian perfection is considered an oddity.

Noah was definitely an oddity. Because of his obedience to God, however, he and his family escaped death. Noah's goal of perfection served him and his family well indeed!

God's plan for animal sacrifice required that the animal be perfect in order to be accepted. A perfect, unblemished sacrifice demonstrated a man's desire to give his very best to God.

God's desire to help those who strive for Christian perfection cannot be overemphasized: "The eyes of the Lord search back and forth across the whole earth, looking for people whose hearts are perfect toward him so that he can show his great power in helping them" (2 Chron. 16:9 TLB). It is extremely important that we strive to achieve the goals He sets for us. It is not an overstatement to suggest that the problems of this troubled world are the result of our refusal to seek God's goal of perfection.

Jesus re-emphasized God's desire for our perfection: "Be ye therefore perfect, even as your Father which is in heaven is perfect" (Mt. 5:48 KJV). The idea of striving for perfection is unpopular because it seems too difficult to attain or even imagine. But our goal must be to become more like our Teacher who said: "When fully trained, every disciple will be like his teacher" (Lu. 6:40 NAB). To become more like Him we must endeavor to be a "fully trained" disciple! Paul charged every Christian to **aim for perfection**: "Finally, brothers, good-by. Aim for perfection" (2 Cor. 13:11). Yes, many Christians think immoral thoughts; still, we must strive for, and reach for, perfection. Otherwise, we can never become all God has called us to be. My heart rejoices that we can learn to have thoughts that please God! *Strategy #8* – Seek for perfection.

Our high calling is recorded in 1 Peter 1:15: "as he who called you is holy, so be holy in all you do." This is such a demanding challenge that our fallen nature can easily persuade us to ignore it: "It's too difficult. So if it's too difficult, why even bother to try?" And, after all, disregarding it leaves us free to do things that we know are wrong! Satan encourages this kind of thinking, so Christians are often unaware that they are justifying the things they choose to do. Because of this, we get into serious problems and then wonder why they happened. Satan makes it easy for us to get into trouble – all we need to do is listen to his thoughts and close our minds to the warnings the Scriptures give us.

Our conscience causes us to feel guilty when we think immoral thoughts. This inner warning is a God-given treasure. It reflects the warning: "Be careful how you think. Your life is shaped by your **thoughts**" (Prov. 4:23 GN). *Strategy #9* – Pay close attention to your conscience.

Our conscience is God's instrument to help us become the holy people that He called us to be (see Lev. 20:7). He doesn't automatically change us from our old disobedient selves, but He makes it possible for us to live lives that are "leading to holiness" (see Rom 6:19). Unless we pay close attention to this calling, we will find it easy to do what *we* want rather than what *He* wants. God does not make the changes in us that *we* need to make! We need to obey Him and *then* He will help us to: "Hate what is evil" (Rom. 12:9). This is no easy task when immoral desires are involved! Our natural mind tends to love, rather than hate, immorality.

After I learned to close my eyes to whatever stimulated immoral thoughts, I was amazed as

God's miracle began working in me. Scenes that previously had captivated my thoughts, I began to hate. I sensed that God's hate for evil was actually working in me! Absolutely amazing. Slowly, but surely, I was understanding what it means to have thoughts that are pleasing to God.

To help us have a clearer understanding of the way God thinks, in comparison to the ways we like to think, the Bible gives us an illustration. God says that as the heavens are higher than the earth, so His thoughts are higher than ours. The *nearest* star is 3.4 light-years away, which is equal to around *twenty-four* trillion miles. That is indeed high above the earth! Even without a telescope we can see stars that are two million light years away from earth. But even that is close to earth compared to one distant galaxy seen by the Hubble telescope. It is ten to fourteen billion light-years away from earth!

Of course, we can't really understand these huge distances, but it helps us understand how diligent we must be in trying to have thoughts that will please God.

Paul understood that our bodies want to control our thoughts: "Dear brothers, I plead with you to give your bodies to God. Let them be a living sacrifice, holy – the kind he can accept. When you think of what he has done for you, is this too much to ask?" (Rom 12:1 TLB).

Paul is pleading with us to sacrifice our own desires so we can become the holy people God wants us to be.

Our fallen nature does not want to admit that it is in rebellion against God. It prefers to remain free to gratify itself while ignoring God's will. We can be disobeying God, all the while denying our guilt. Parents have observed this behavior in children. The parent is certain that a child has been disobedient, but the child emphatically denies he did anything improper.

Imagine that you are blessed with a 250-pound, 6-foot 3-inch body, and you passionately want to play professional football. But what must you do in order to reach that goal? Exert a tremendous amount of effort? Yes, and then some. Becoming a professional football player requires intense determination and work, work, work. It requires a man to strain with all his might and deny himself many things he would never be willing to give up if it were not for his desire to succeed. The same is true for a man who wants to be obedient to God's Word in Ephesians 5:3: "Among you there must not be even a hint of sexual immorality, or of any kind of impurity." God has called us and has given us the power to be His holy people. But we must do whatever is necessary to become that person. We must strive to defeat any "hint of sexual immorality" or "any kind of impurity." If we fail to respond to God's *call*, we should expect His *discipline*.

Colossians 3:5 gives us specific instructions: "Put to death, therefore, whatever belongs to your earthly nature: sexual immorality, impurity, lust, evil desires." This exhortation makes it clear that we are dealing with a very serious subject.

Our thoughts exert such a powerful influence over the things we will eventually *do*, that the Bible exhorts us to take the forceful action of putting to death our earthly nature. If we choose to deal with our natural desires in a careless, half-hearted way, those desires will continue to control our thoughts and, sooner or later, the things we do. All our good intentions will be futile until we take action – determined action – to destroy the sinful desires that churn in our hearts and minds. We must not indulge desires that we are told to *put to death! Strategy #10* – Exercise discipline over your desires.

It takes only a second to turn our eyes away from things that might stimulate immoral thoughts, but it will take us much longer to learn how to always choose pure thoughts. Any man who dares to challenge his own evil desires will find that he is in for a real battle. First Peter 2:11 tells us to: "abstain from sinful **desires**, which war against your soul." This war is raging even now, yet the problem is that countless men are unaware of it! We must make ourselves aware, if we are to put our sinful desires to death.

When we accept Jesus as our Savior, we receive God's free gift of eternal life. From then on we are called to strive to become more like Jesus. This should be our number one goal. God's goodness *teaches* us, but it is *we* who must do the learning! We begin that process when we say "No" to our passions.

Most of us require much soul searching to even *want* to live a Christ-like life! Our success depends on how great our desire is to succeed. So be warned: Living a Christ-like life will require more persistence, more determination than would be required to become a professional sports player. But many men do not realize how much strength they can muster when they set their wills to follow Christ's example. This is where persistent determination becomes vital, for when we become a Christian, our sinful nature does not immediately desire to be like Christ. Rather, our fallen nature wants to continue to gratify the desires of our sinful nature.

Since the fall of the human race, one of the strongest natural desires that men have is the desire to lust after women. This desire is so strong that men find it incredibly difficult to overcome. This causes an intense conflict within most Christian men, but there is a solution: We must strive to change our natural desires! This is perhaps the most difficult challenge we will ever face, but *with God's help we can do it!*

Ephesians 4:22 commands us to: "Put off your old self, which is being corrupted by its deceitful **desires**." Once again, determination will be required, but with Christ's help we can do this!

The story of Samson provides a revealing, real-life example of what happens when we succumb to our sinful desires. Samson allowed himself to be seduced by the beautiful temptress Delilah, and revealed to her the secret of his strength. One night, as he slept, Delilah cut his long hair and God's presence and strength left him. When we indulge our sinful desires, God's strength and protection will eventually leave us and great suffering will surely follow. Like Sampson, we can be blissfully unaware that God's Holy Spirit has ceased to convict us – until we have fallen into Satan's trap.

Rebellion against God and its consequent suffering are increasing dramatically throughout our land. This tragic trend will continue unless a spiritual awakening touches the hearts of our people. A newscast I saw recently illustrated the decadence and depravity that infects the minds of our youth and provided a shocking example of the destruction of our moral fiber.

About one hundred college students were

gathered at a popular bar to celebrate spring break. As the camera rolled, young men and women hoisted mugs of beer to their lips and drained the contents in mere seconds.

The camera shifted to another section of the bar where a group of drunken male students had placed a female student on a table. As the men stripped the clothing from the grinning young woman, the men sprayed whipped cream over various parts of her body. The spectators gathered around and cheered their approval.

Then the group of men began to lick the whipped cream from the woman's body. The grins on the faces of the besotted participants and spectators alike revealed that they thought this was great sport. Could Sodom and Gomorrah have been any worse?

The same telecast reported that in recent years more and more young people have become addicted to illegal drugs, have contracted incurable diseases, and are committing suicide in greater and greater numbers. These tragedies should alert us that our once strong moral fiber is rapidly tearing apart.

Are you fighting to resist immoral thoughts, or are you succumbing easily to them? If you are not resisting, you will not be able to help yourself, or anyone else, win this spiritual battle. Like Samson, you will awaken one day and realize that God has allowed you to lose your spiritual strength. When we fully understand what God thinks about immoral thoughts we will abhor what we once enjoyed.

The rapid increase in the spread of AIDS paints a sobering portrait of things to come for a world that is placing sexual gratification at the top of its priorities. A United Nations report says that during 1980 to 2000, twenty-two million people worldwide have died from this disease, and that the numbers of cases are rising dramatically. In one country in Africa alone, one-third of the adult population is afflicted with this incurable, deadly disease, and even that alarming percentage is still increasing. When God withdraws His presence from any people, the results are devastating. Can this happen here in the United States? Absolutely! Never before has our nation been in such great need for God's supernatural protection. Many strong nations, throughout history, have fallen as a direct result of moral failures. If we Christians want God to move on our behalf, we should stay as far away as possible from any form of immorality.

Chapter 12

The Power of Temptation

You have heard people from other nations speak English with varying degrees of proficiency. Despite having struggled for years to learn all the subtle nuances of this difficult language, many are still unable to articulate as well as they would like. Learning to think pure thoughts might be equally difficult for you, but with persistence and God's help, you *can* learn a new way of thinking.

If you have practiced immoral thinking for years, it may be difficult for you to understand *how* to have pure thoughts. The director of the French Language Program at U.C. Irvine, CA, says, "You can't compartmentalize a language. You have to be in a context where you live in that language, and where you even dream in that language. Speaking an hour a week can't produce that." The director recommends that a dedicated language student move to the country where that particular language is spoken and submerge himself in the normal activities of an average citizen. To learn the language of the Holy Spirit (to learn to think pure thoughts), we must find ways to submerge ourselves in *His* way of thinking. *Strategy #11* – Find ways to cause yourself to think as God thinks.

Morally pure thoughts are very high on God's list of priorities. Jesus said: "Blessed are the pure in heart for they will see God" (Mt. 5:8). Can there be a greater, more exciting goal than to *see God?*

If a reformed alcoholic spends an evening in a bar, he may or may not relapse into drinking. If he spends many evenings in a bar, the odds are high that he will end up drunk. If a forgiven adulterer permits himself to stare at something that *might* give him immoral thoughts, he will probably end up thinking immoral thoughts. If he persistently looks at something that arouses his immoral desires, he will once again **be** an adulterer in his heart. Just as an alcoholic should not expose himself to alcohol or to those who consume it, a forgiven adulterer should not expose his eyes to anything that might tempt him.

On the eve of His crucifixion, Jesus told Peter: "Watch and pray, lest you enter into temptation. The spirit indeed is willing, but the flesh is weak" (Mt. 26:41 (NKJV). The temptation to think immoral thoughts may be the worst and most frequent problem in your life. If you are not actively praying to be led out of these seductive thoughts, you could continue in them for the rest of your life! No matter how close we are to Christ, we, like Peter, are still subject to temptation. We need to watch and pray lest we fall under the temptations that come to us nearly every day, and sometimes every hour.

We men all too often behave like the man described in Proverbs 7:22: "He followed her like an ox going to the slaughter, like a deer stepping into a noose." What a clear picture! An unwary animal walks willingly to its slaughter, unaware that it will soon become ensnared and die. An unwary man can follow this same fatal course and walk blindly into his own destruction. He thought he was clever when he convinced the woman to have an affair with him, but both persons ended up with their lives a disaster.

Solomon, the wisest man who ever lived, offered young men this advice: "Listen to me, young men, and not only listen but obey; don't let your desires get out of hand; don't let yourself **think** about her. Don't go near her; stay away from where she walks (*or appears in pictures or film*!), lest she temp you and seduce you. For she has been the ruin of multitudes – a vast host of men have been her victims" (Prov. 7:23-27 TLB).

Millions of men have proven these verses to be true, but you do not need to add yourself to the list. You will, however, if you let your "desires get out of hand."

Some young men may dismiss this wise advice and think, *When I get older I will not be so severely tempted to have immoral thoughts.* Unfortunately that is not the case. Sin, by its nature, grows progressively stronger. The more we indulge in sexual fantasies, the more tightly we become ensnared in their addictive grip. Eventually we reach the state of: "Having lost all sensitivity, they have given themselves over to sensuality so as to indulge in every kind of impurity, with a continual lust for more" (Eph. 4:19).

A dangerous part of our human nature is that we often think we can get away with enjoying whatever we want to enjoy – even after we've seen a mountain of evidence proving that others have suffered greatly when they did the same thing. If a man deliberately injures his body, we think he is foolish. It is equally foolish for a Christian to injure himself by practicing a sin that God has promised to punish.

Satan uses many devious methods to convince us that immoral thoughts are "only natural" and that God isn't likely to punish us for being "only human." Satan is also very skillful at presenting immoral thoughts as being too enjoyable to be evil. Romans 12:1 (NKJV) tells us what is merely our *reasonable* service to God: "I beseech you therefore, brethren, by the mercies of God, that you present your bodies a living sacrifice, holy, acceptable to God, which is your reasonable service." Not extraordinarily fine service, just "reasonable service."

The spirit of Christ that came to dwell in us when we were born again has the power to help us give "reasonable service" to God. Our "body," which includes our natural desires, does not want to become anything even remotely holy. Rather, its natural desire is for everything that is unholy. The world certainly does not conform to God's will. Rather, it works incessantly to get us to conform to its behavior. Yet, through Jesus, we can be transformed and our minds renewed.

Every temptation is accompanied by a host of reasons why it is perfectly all right to submit to it. But James 4:17 tells us that if we know what is good, but do something else, we are sinning. The Greek word for "good," also means, "right thing." Once we know what the *right* thing is, but fail to do it, to us that is sin. Do you know that it is *wrong* to look at a woman and think lustful thoughts? If not, read Matthew 5:28 once again:

"But I tell you that anyone who looks at a woman lustfully has already committed adultery with her in his heart."

Jesus made it clear that if we do what He told us is wrong; we have no excuse for committing that sin (see Jn. 15:22). I have spoken with many Christian men regarding their immoral thoughts and to a man, each has admitted that he knew his thoughts were wrong. How dangerous it is for us to know God's will yet still find excuses to disobey Him! God is a forgiving God and a God of grace. But we should not trifle with His grace. Only His mercy causes Him to give us ample opportunity to change our ways.

Gaining control over our immoral thoughts will not be easy, but 2 Corinthians 10:5 tells us to: "Take captive **every thought** to make it obedient to Christ." It is our responsibility however to "take them captive." Too often men and women confess their immoral thoughts to God, but then do nothing to cause their thoughts to become "obedient to Christ." Some think their disobedience to God is merely a personal weakness that someday, somehow they will overcome. But immoral thoughts come directly from Satan, which is why James 4:7 tells us to: "Resist the devil." When we do: "He will flee from us." Remember, every time Satan tempts us to linger upon something that creates immoral desires in us, we are being drawn by his evil power. Just as he twisted scripture to tempt Jesus, Satan manipulates scripture to try to make us believe that there is little we can do to change ourselves. For example, Satan might quote 2 Corinthians 5:17 (KJV): "If any man be in Christ, he is a new creature: old things are passed away; behold, all things are become new." Satan would have us believe that Christ has already done in us everything that needs to be done, so there is nothing left for *us* to do. He, and our natural minds, wants us to ignore: "I can do all things through Christ who strengthens me" (Phil. 4:13 NKJV).

God used this verse as an important insight that helped me understand how I could be delivered from the curse of immoral thoughts. Because Christ lives in us, we *can* do all things, even things our natural minds tell us are impossible! Not only *can* we, we *must* if we want to be pleasing to God. *Strategy #12* – Believe Christ gives you His strength.

What happens when we disregard God's pleas for us to obey Him rather than our own desires? Ezekiel 11:21 speaks of "vile images and detestable idols." Here in modern America most of us do not worship images or idols of stone, but we do worship idols made of flesh. Sex and sexual innuendo reign supreme in our culture. Our movies, magazines, television, advertisements and clothing flagrantly promote and glorify sex. Ezekiel 22:4 says: "You have become . . . defiled by the idols you have made."

SECRET SINS

Chapter 13

The Choice of Punishment

Parents use two main methods to get children to obey them: punishment and reward. God uses similar methods with His children. We choose which method we want Him to use. He promises to judge every person and to give us what we deserve (see Rom. 2:5, 6).

There are those who have received God's free gift of eternal life, but have forgotten, or choose to ignore, the fact that He is also just. When we come to Him He adopts us as His children and promises to treat us as any loving parent would treat his children – with love, and with discipline. First Corinthians 6:9 (TLB) warns us: "Don't fool yourselves. Those who live immoral lives . . . will have no share in his Kingdom." This should leave us no doubt about how God views immorality. We may fool ourselves into thinking that our thoughts and actions will not affect our "share" in His Kingdom, but His Words tell us otherwise. Hebrews 13:4 adds: "God will judge the adulterer and all the sexually immoral." Unless we obtain

God's forgiveness, we will, at some time and in some way, suffer for our immorality.

Romans 2:9 explains what may await us: "There will be trouble and distress for every human being who does evil." The Greek word that is translated here as *trouble*, also means: afflictions, anguish and distress. Think of all the afflictions, anguish and distress that will come to us if we disregard God's will!

Now, what will happen to those who: "have escaped the corruption of the world by knowing our Lord and Savior Jesus Christ and are again entangled in it and overcome?" (2 Pet. 2:20). I phrase this question, "What would happen to me, Merlin, if I should become "entangled and overcome?" Verse 21 provides a clear answer: "It would have been better for them not to have known the way of righteousness." What a sobering statement! It is of vital importance that you avoid entangling yourself in the corruption of the world!

God, our Creator, punishes sin. Ample evidence is seen throughout the world. His methods of punishment are diverse and well recorded in Scripture. It is impossible to escape His discipline for our sin unless we have the kind of sorrow God wants his people to have. We may feel *sorrow* because we have sinned, but there is a sharp difference between the Greek word, *lupe*, for sorrow, and the Greek word, *eis mentanoian* meaning "into repentance." It is quite clear in the original language that sorrow, alone, is *not* repentance. The word for repentance means, "**changing our thought pattern**!"

Of course, we may be sorry because our sins have been uncovered, but there is another kind of sorrow, a Godly sorrow that causes us to change the way we think. When we truly become eager to get rid of sin in our lives, we can then benefit from the results of Godly sorrow.

We Christians must heighten our awareness of what is going on in the world around us because a spiritual battle is raging. Remember Esau who sold his inheritance rights for a single meal? Men and women frequently sell their "happiness inheritance" for a single immoral act, and then experience a lifetime of regret. We can come to our senses and escape from any carefully devised ambush set by our enemy. Second Timothy 3 warns us that there will be *terrible times* in the last days. People will be lovers of themselves and lovers of pleasure rather than lovers of God. If we have loved pleasure more than God we need to follow the example of the prophet Jeremiah. He recognized what he had done as a young man, and was ashamed and humiliated (see Jer. 31:19).

Since God is a God of love as well as discipline, He will provide ample opportunity for every man to repent and be completely forgiven. But take heed: If we have repented but then continue to repeat the same sins, we are in grave danger.

If you habitually think immoral thoughts it is very likely the way you have conditioned your mind to think. For example, when a beautiful woman, or her picture, appears before your eyes, you have before that moment already established what you will think and desire. When you hear or see the word "sex," your mind replays whatever scenarios have been pre-recorded on it. Different people replay different memories. A woman who has been raped may feel anger, fear or pain upon hearing or seeing the word. An adult who was molested as a child might experience a similar reaction. In short, the word, or idea of, "sex," will cause whatever image or feeling that person's mind has been trained to think or feel. God has given us the capacity to renew our minds, which, in turn, enables us to reprogram our reaction to every kind of situation. The choice is ours, but if we choose to cling to our old, immoral patterns of thought, God will never grant us deliverance from His just discipline!

How might God punish us for our transgressions against His laws? Are you willing to take your chances with a God who loves you enough to punish you? In Ezekiel 38:4 (TLB) God warns: "I will put hooks into your jaws." Sounds painful! In Amos 2 God speaks of people who have sinned again and again. He warns them that He will not forget that they are refusing to obey Him.

But we can have the joy of obeying Him!

Our flesh is often unwilling to give up forbidden pleasures until it is confronted with convincing evidence that it will suffer because of them. It's easy to think that God will never hold us accountable for our immoral thoughts, so we continue to enjoy them until some catastrophic event reveals that we were wrong. People smoked cigarettes for many years without seeing any evidence that they were endangering their health. Then, all at once, their sentence was announced: debilitating illness and slow, painful death.

If God decides to punish us He can merely withdraw His protective hand. All He has to do is allow Satan to do what he already wants to do. And Satan, as we know, will eagerly and gleefully attack us.

I sometimes shudder when I consider the multitude of afflictions that Satan could inflict upon our bodies! Once God has given him permission to do so, it is then too late for us to wish we had listened more carefully to His instructions.

King David disregarded God's laws, suffered, and then wrote: "I am listening carefully to all the Lord is saying" (Ps. 85:8 TLB). God is not eager to punish His people. Just the opposite!

He yearns to help us so we will not destroy ourselves. It was for this reason the He gave us His Word, where His will for us is clearly spelled out.

When the woman who had been caught in adultery was brought to Jesus, He revealed God's compassionate nature – He forgave her. God wants to forgive you and me for all our sins, too, but He also wants us to heed Jesus' admonition to the woman. His instruction was simple – stop sinning!

Like it or not: "The day will surely come when our inmost thoughts will be revealed" (Rom. 2:16 TLB). What a dreadful thought! Imagine your most secret, intimate thoughts revealed for all to see. But God announced this event long ago, so we should not be surprised when it occurs. But there is hope, for we know that: "Godly sorrow brings repentance that leads to salvation" (2 Cor. 7:10). The fact that we will one day stand before Christ to be judged for all our "inmost thoughts," is a most urgent reason for us to frequently repeat, and earnestly desire the prayer in Psalm 51:10 (TLB): "Create in me a new, clean heart, O God, filled with clean **thoughts** and right **desires**."

Any relationship based on immorality is inevitably destined to bring heartache to one or both persons. At first, both parties may anticipate an enjoyable, exciting, passionate experience, but *anything* based on disobedience to

God will always result in suffering. Always! Even a marriage that is based solely on sexual gratification will fail. Why? Because God created and intended for His holy union to be based on much more than mere physical attraction. Many couples in our secular society would be surprised to learn that a marriage that follows the Biblical rules, will give both husband and wife a happy and fulfilling marriage.

At one time the United States decided that slavery was not evil. Slavery was practiced for generations as our citizens disregarded the Golden Rule. In order to justify themselves, some men believed that black people were not humans – end of discussion. Some slave owners treated their slaves more humanely than others, and thus excused themselves. God did nothing to make it obvious that slavery would be punished, so the practice continued. But then hundreds of thousands of people died in the terrible, bloody Civil War.

Hitler brought great prosperity to Germany. The people loved all the affluence that he brought to them. Then Hitler declared that certain people did not have the right to live and set out to murder millions of them. Since most people were prosperous, they looked the other way, and evil reigned.

God permitted Hitler and his followers to wreck havoc on many millions of people – as evil thrived. *But God's laws had been broken.* Then came the horrors of the bloodiest and most destructive war in history. When finally, mercifully, the frenzied bloodletting was over, millions of people had perished.

To this day I remember walking through German cities following the war. In some cities nearly every building had been demolished. I watched in silence as haggard, bone-thin women picked eagerly through garbage discarded by our soldiers. And strewn all around me were the twisted, still smoking ruins of great buildings where a proud people had once lived. Once again sin had inflicted retribution on a nation.

Immoral thoughts and their subsequent actions have brought suffering and death to millions of people. Christians, we urgently need to remember that God's wrath is often slow to come, but it *will* come. God Himself warned: "Be sure your sin will find you out" (Num. 32:23 KJV). If we have disobeyed His laws, we must repent. That is, *change our way of thinking*!

Jesus' parable of the tares (weeds) shows that God does not always destroy evil before His harvest time comes: "Let both grow together until the harvest. At that time I will tell the harvesters: First collect the weeds and tie them in bundles to be burned" (Mt. 13:30). In verse 41 Jesus speaks about the end times as He explains the manner in which God will carry out His justice. He will: "Weed out of his kingdom everything that causes sin and all who do evil." Then verse 57 says: "They took offense at him." People were offended when Jesus said things they didn't like. People today also take offense when told they must control their thought life if they do not want to suffer God's discipline.

There is nothing in the New Testament that suggests that we Christians can carelessly skip through life with no punishment for our disobedience of God's moral laws. The truth, in fact is exactly the opposite! In this life or in eternity, we will experience the consequences of how we have lived. No man can know *how* God will do this, but be assured that He will keep His promise to execute His righteous judgment. At that time we will be fully convinced that His judgment is righteous. The desire for immoral thoughts is often so strong that we may be tempted to disregard the consequences. But if we *really* consider the potential results, our conduct will likely be much different.

Think of what it would be like if there were no laws against robbing a bank. What if anyone could enter a bank and simply help himself to all those appealing piles of money. But there are laws against theft. There are man's laws and God's laws. The wise man would not rob a bank because man's law would severely punish him. The moral, God-fearing man would not steal the money because *God* would punish him. Fear of punishment, then, would deter both men.

Proverbs 6:25 gives us a clear warning: "Do not lust in your heart after her beauty or let her captivate you with her eyes." God has so clearly forbidden men to lust after women that we have no reason to think we will not eventually suffer if we disobey Him. Verse 27 adds: "Can a man scoop fire into his lap without his clothes being burned?" If immoral thoughts produced the nearly instant result that being burned does, we might not yield to temptation as easily as we do. But our thoughts can produce results that are far more damaging to us than fire.

Many men look upon women as something like a dessert buffet. If a woman looks good, they want to sample her to see how enjoyable she might be. If the woman appears to be especially desirable, some men will want her regardless of what it might cost them. But no one is able to predict how painful the consequences might be.

God has given us a conscience that helps us to discern right from wrong. Consider this scenario. If your wife, daughter, sister or mother were attacked by a rapist, would you do everything in your power to stop the rapist or would you turn your back so you wouldn't have to watch? Most of us know exactly what we would do. We have an inner, God-given knowledge that we should, and would, fight to protect our loved one from being molested. But why is this so important to us? Because we know instinctively that sex is wrong if not used correctly. How would you react if a rapist were attacking a woman you do not know? Most of us would still use every means available to stop the attack.

How would you react if your wife, daughter, sister or mother were being forced to disrobe and be photographed – not raped – just photographed? Most of us know that we would still react with whatever means we had available. In our hearts, we really believe that such things are wrong. But if we see a photograph of a naked woman who is unknown to us, our corrupted conscience may accept and even permit us to enjoy it.

What if your mother, sister or daughter had an especially voluptuous body and agreed to be photographed for a centerfold magazine? Would you hang her picture on your wall for others to enjoy? Not likely. You would be ashamed of the picture and not want others to see it. Why is that? Because we still have within us some of the feelings and instincts that God created in His original creation. We still know that certain things are wrong and should not be enjoyed. God sees every girl and woman as deserving of respect and protection, and He is angered by anyone who treats her as if she were only a beautiful animal.

Notice that evil spirits always had to do exactly what Jesus told them to do. But when God created mankind in His image, He gave us free will. This free will enables us to disregard whatever He tells us to do. But there are *always* consequences to our thoughts and actions. We may think we are getting away with disobedience, but eventually we will reap what we have sown.

King Herod believed that John the Baptist was a holy man, so he wished no harm to come to him. But Herod made the same mistake that many men make; he looked at and enjoyed the sexy behavior of a beautiful young woman – Herodias' daughter. Then she named her price – the head of John the Baptist. This consequence was far higher than Herod had expected, but he was trapped. Many men have been trapped by the price of immoral desires. A single mistake can cause us to suffer for the rest of our lives. We Christian men should draw a lesson from Herod's experience. We, too, may be on the brink of making the same costly and painful mistake, blissfully unaware that we are bringing forth our own destruction.

Second Samuel 11:2 offers another compelling example of the dire consequences of lustful desires: "One evening David got up from his bed and walked around on the roof of the palace. From the roof he saw a woman bathing. The woman was very beautiful." David **looked**, and desire stirred within him. And as it often does, *his desire* caused his actions.

Retribution is sure to come to those who disobey God. Eventually David shed bitter, anguished tears as he begged God to forgive his sins of adultery and murder. Nevertheless, David's child died – David had looked first, and then acted on his desires.

The broken and repentant David cried: "Before I was afflicted I went astray, but now I obey your word" (Ps.119:67). God will often allow suffering and tragedy to come to us, or those we love, because He knows such pain will get our attention. But why wait until God afflicts us, or those we love? Why not ask Him to help us change from what we are to what we should be?

When we give in to our craving for lustful thoughts, we are putting God to the test. Unless we repent and forsake our defiance, we, like David, will ultimately be punished. We must strive, then, to turn away from temptation.

If our hearts desire is to *disobey* God, it will be very difficult for us to obey Him. But when our desire is to please Him, He will help us to be obedient.

In Psalm 50 David speaks of men who:

"throw in their lot with adulterers." Few Christian men would be willing to acknowledge that they "throw in their lot with adulterers," but that is exactly what we do if we indulge in looking at images that glamorize immorality. However, God shows us a way out of such moral failures. He tells us to: "Hate evil, love good" (Amos 5:15).

Our enjoyment of evil would be radically reduced were we to ponder the lesson in Numbers 25:1-11. The men of Israel were having immoral sexual relations with Moabite women who invited them to join in their sacrifices to Baal. God told Moses to kill the leaders who were guilty of this. But instead of repenting: "An Israelite man brought to his family a Midianite woman right before the eyes of Moses and the whole assembly of Israel while they were weeping at the entrance to the Tent of Meeting. When Phinehas . . . saw this, he left the assembly, took a spear in his hand and followed the Israelite into the tent. He drove the spear through both of them . . . Then the plague against the Israelites was stopped; but those who died in the plague numbered 24,000. The LORD said to Moses, "Phinehas . . . has turned my anger away from the Israelites; for he was as zealous as I am for my honor among them, so that in my zeal I did not put an end to them." God's wrath can, and will, be aroused against those who misuse the sexual urges He gave us. He caused 24,000 people to die because men were involved in sexual sin. Surely we should learn that immorality is not the innocent sport that some are now attempting to portray it as being.

God's anger toward sexual sin sometimes comes quickly, sometimes not. But whether His punishment comes swiftly, or many years later, His word assures us that it *will* come!

Solomon wrote: "I find more bitter than death, the woman who is a snare . . .The man who pleases God will escape her, but the sinner she will ensnare" (Eccl. 7:26). Young women learn quickly today that if they dress in a provocative manner they can attract a man's notice. They may be unaware that in God's eyes their provocative appearance is "more bitter than death."

For the young man, youth seems that it will go on and on, but eventually youth fades away. Immoral thoughts may go on and on, but unlike youth, they don't fade away. Disobedience of God's commands will eventually bring consequences. That is an absolute fact that we can count on.

Christians who have never learned to submit to God's authority often rebel against Him. But just as Adam and Eve suffered for their rebellion, every Christian will suffer if he uses his eyes and thoughts as instruments to disobey God. Such rebellion is a choice. Immoral thoughts don't "just happen," they are **nurtured** and **entertained** in our hearts, where, if we are not vigilant, they will grow in frequency and strength.

I know from personal experience that it is disastrous for a Christian to abandon his desire to live a life that is pleasing to God. That is precisely what happened to me when I served in the Army during World War II. During that period of my life I made mistakes that caused me great suffering for many years. Eventually God helped me, but only after allowing me to suffer for those many years. Now I see more clearly why it is disastrous to stray from God's will.

Chapter 14

The Choice of Rewards!

An overcomer is someone who triumphs over something. God has called us to triumph over the forces that tempt us to be disobedient to Him. Revelation 2:26 tells us: "To him who overcomes and does my will to the end, I will give authority over the nations." What wonderful challenges and opportunities we have! Just as God gave Jesus authority because He overcame temptations, Jesus will give us authority if we overcome ours!

Revelation 3:21 gives us this incredible promise: "To him who overcomes, I will give the right to sit with me on my throne, just as I overcame and sat down with my Father on his throne." If we are overcomers we will be honored in Heaven!

Jesus was the first overcomer; He calls us to follow His example. He made it possible for us to defeat temptation, but first we must believe that He gives us this power. Those who will not believe Him will suffer the consequences of their unbelief. They will, inevitably, be overcome by the world.

If we do not want to be overcome by the world, we must strive to allow more of Christ's nature to work in us. Luke 8 tells us that demons fell screaming in terror before Jesus. If we want demons to feel comfortable in our presence, we need only have unholy thoughts living in us. The mark of an overcomer, after all, is one whose thoughts are pleasing to God: "The Lord detests the thoughts of the wicked, but those of the pure are pleasing to him" (Prov. 15:26).

There have always been strict standards regarding the gifts God will accept from His people. Crippled or diseased animals were never acceptable sacrifices. If improper animal sacrifices were not acceptable to God, why should Christians think we could offer Him our gifts of praise and worship, while at the same time clinging to the immorality in our hearts? Surely God does not find such offerings acceptable.

For the past two thousand years, dedicated Christians have taught that mankind's salvation depends on faith in Christ, not on man's good works. This emphasis has been necessary because many people have believed that they can purchase their salvation through their own good deeds. But the emphasis on faith for salvation has caused some Christians to ignore the reality that – in eternity – God will reward *everything* we do for Him.

Once we accept the reality that we cannot earn our salvation through good works, we may find it easy to think, *Good works aren't important.* But this would be a serious mistake, because we are: "created in Christ Jesus to do good works, which God prepared in advance for us to do" (Eph. 2:10)! God gives us His free gift of eternal life in order that we might then serve Him. And He has promised to richly reward our service!

In His parable of the talents (Mt. 25), Jesus speaks of servants who received talents from their master, before he went away. When the master returned to "settle accounts," each servant was rewarded or punished according to how well he had used that which had been entrusted to him. Jesus was clearly warning us that we will be held accountable for how well we use the talents and abilities that He has given us!

Throughout the Bible God stresses the importance of our thoughts: "Cleanse your **minds** and **hearts**, not just your bodies, or else my anger will burn you to a crisp because of all your sins. And no one will be able to put the fire out . . . You can yet be saved by casting out your evil **thoughts**" (Jer. 4:4, 14 TLB). We all want to be rewarded by God, but let's not be deceived into thinking, *Since I'm a Christian, God won't punish me for my disobedience to His* *will.* God knows and understands our weaknesses, but remember: "It is not those who **hear** the law who are righteous in God's sight, but it is those who **obey** the law who will be declared righteous" (Rom. 2:13).

It is logical, and scriptural, that in Heaven men will be rewarded according to the good they have done: "When the Lord comes, he will turn on the light so that everyone can see exactly what each one of us is really like, deep down in our hearts . . . At that time God will give to each one whatever praise is coming to him" (1 Cor. 4:5 TLB).

We will not be rewarded for the things we **fail** to do!

First Corinthians 9:24 adds: "In a race all the runners run, but only one gets the prize. Run in such a way as to get the prize." Paul was determined to run his race with all the zeal he could muster! He was determined to win his prize! You and I must decide if we are that interested in winning any of God's special prizes.

Winning "the race" to serve and obey God requires much more than merely a vague desire to be pleasing to Him. To win this race we must deny ourselves many things that would make us "feel good." An athlete denies himself many things just to win a medal, but we do this for a heavenly reward that will never disappear!

God has His own plan for rewarding us. He

promises not to judge us by our outward appearances, but by our *thoughts* and *intentions* (see 1 Sam. 16:7). The recently invented Total Body Scanner gives us some idea of how God probes into and sees our thoughts and intentions. The Body Scanner can see every joint, organ and muscle of the human body. God, in His wisdom, can see every thought, idea and attitude of the human mind. We can only hide our *Secret Sins* from others – never from God.

James and John asked Jesus: "Let one of us sit at your right and the other at your left in your glory" (Mk. 10:37). Their desire to be near to Jesus revealed their love for Him, but Jesus told them that only His Father could make that decision. Jesus' response makes it clear that some people will be nearer to Him in Heaven than others.

Is it your desire to have a place in Heaven near Jesus? I don't mean to have a position of power or prestige, but to be near Him. When God looks at your heart, does He see you as one of those who hunger and thirst for righteousness? If so, rejoice! The Kingdom of Heaven will be yours! If not, perhaps impure thoughts and intentions are weighing you down, causing you to fall behind in the race you once were determined to win.

Paul was so determined to win his own spiritual battle to be an overcomer that he said: "I beat my body and make it my slave so that after I have preached to others, I myself will not be disqualified for the prize" (1 Cor. 9:27).

Are you *really* determined to be an overcomer? If so, you must keep your eye on the prize, never allowing the desires of your carnal nature to impose their will on you.

It is no easy battle to force your body and mind to submit to God's will, but the prize is *worth every effort* we can make.

The Prodigal Son had spent his entire inheritance on prostitutes and other pleasures, but when he returned home his father welcomed him with open arms. The father's warm welcome is often used as an illustration of God's forgiving grace. Yet it is seldom mentioned that the father said to the elder brother: "Everything I have is yours" (Lu. 15:31). The Prodigal was still a son, but the entire inheritance went to the *faithful* son!

Jesus urged us to store up treasures in Heaven. *All* our efforts to please God are recorded in Heaven! He rewards those who obey His moral laws, and He will recompense each person according to what He sees in our hearts. God would not promise to reward true righteousness if He had no intention of doing so. But we must be especially careful that our pride does not cause us to consider ourselves more worthy of God's rewards than other Christians! Pride in our own merits is poison to the soul.

Many Christians have died after years of suffering, with little evidence that God had even noticed their service to Him. But God promised that in Heaven: "Each will receive his own reward according to his own labor" (1 Cor. 3:8 NASB). He has eternity in which He can keep this promise. In Heaven: "Each of us will give an account of himself to God" (Rom. 14:12). Since God says our immoral thoughts are adultery, we must be prepared to account for those thoughts when we stand before Him to be judged.

When we are enjoying immoral thoughts we are not likely to think of ourselves as being sinful. But we are not the final judges of our own acts. First John 3:1-2 (TLB) says: "Everyone who really believes this will try to stay pure because Christ is pure" (1 Jn. 3:1-2 TLB). If our goal is to become like Christ we must try to "stay pure" because Christ is pure.

Do you understand this? Are you striving to be pure like Christ? Will you let the way Christ thought become the way you think?

Most of us understand that if we are a good Christian now, that will help us to have a happier life, but Paul assures us that the way we live in this life can help us to be happier in eternity! And because he knows this to be true, he urges us to keep a close watch on all our **thoughts** (see 1 Tim 4:8, 16 TLB). Second Timothy 2:21 sets this goal for us: "If you stay away from sin . . . Christ himself can use you for his highest purposes." What a high calling we have been given!

Chapter 15

Learning How to Have Pure Thoughts

Learning has one major requirement; to learn, we must **want** to be taught. If we really want to learn to have pure thoughts, God will help us make whatever changes we need to make.

James 1:8 (KJV) describes the shameful condition in which Christian men can find themselves: "A double minded man is unstable in all his ways." How does one get into this condition?: "Each one is tempted when, by his own evil desire, he is dragged away and enticed" (Vs 14). Yes, if we are not careful we can be enticed by our own desires! These **desires** must be changed – not just our actions! Otherwise, our evil desires will eventually give birth to evil actions.

Changing our way of thinking about the opposite sex may seem too difficult to achieve, but it *is* possible. Instead of looking at a sexually appealing woman then fighting to keep our desires pure, we can train our eyes to look at whatever will give us good thoughts! We can, and **must** learn to do so.

Remember this – perhaps write it on a 3 x 5 card and refer to it often: *Whatever you think about **is** what you are becoming.*

One way to cultivate the habit of thinking pure thoughts is to *decide in advance* what we will think whenever a seductive image comes into view.

We can resolve to have only pure thoughts. *Strategy #13*:

1. God designed her!
2. God created her!
3. She belongs to God!

Thoughts such as these have profound power. Whoever the woman may be, we know that God designed her, and that she belongs to Him.

Whatever physical attractiveness she may have is because God created her this way!

Heartfelt praise to God for the magnificence of His creation will cut off the evil thoughts that Satan would love to generate in us. A simple prayer such as this can help us resist, and defeat, impure thoughts:

Lord, help her to know and love You. Help her to have a pure heart. Use her to win many people to Christ. Use her to build Your Church and Your Kingdom. Help her to be a blessing to her husband, children and anyone who loves her.

My prayer for an attractive woman has often been, "Bless her, Lord. Make her pleasing to You." As I repeated such prayers, my thought processes began to change! Slowly but surely I realized that I really *did* want her – and every woman – to be pleasing to Him. And I also realized my increasing disapproval of *anything* that might prevent her from being pleasing to God. What a miracle I was enjoying!

God's anger is stirred whenever He sees a woman used in a way that violates *His* purpose for her. Remember that because of impure desires and adultery, thousands of people were killed after escaping their suffering in Egypt. If we could see the staggering amount of agony that God sees being forced upon His creation, we would rise up in outraged fury. Satan, the mastermind of all this suffering, uses people to achieve his evil goals! We, however, can determine that *we* will not be one of those he uses.

The spiritual battles you will wage in your quest to become more pleasing to God may cause you some discouragement, but take heart: Christ will help you resist impure thoughts and, in time, will cause you to think as He did. Only believe that He WILL help you, and then believe that He IS helping you! Hear Paul's prayer for us: "I pray that Christ will be more and more at home in your hearts, living within you as you trust in him" (Eph. 3:17

TLB). This trust in Christ believes that He **will** deliver us from immoral thoughts, and that He is doing so **NOW**.

The only way for Christ to be "at home" in us, however, is for our hearts to yearn for *His* desires. Paul experienced Christ's changing power, and he prayed for us: "That out of his glorious, unlimited resources he will give you the mighty inner strengthening of his Holy Spirit" (Vs.16). Christ will change our immoral sexual appetites if we ask Him to. He is limited only by our sincere desire to be changed. God promised: "I will give you a new heart and put a new spirit in you" (Ezek. 36:26). The "new heart" God wants to give us, plus His "mighty inner strengthening," makes Christ more and more at home in our hearts!

Unless our hearts and minds are morally clean, we can never hope to wage an effective and lasting campaign against evil. I call upon you, then, to enlist into the army of men who are striving to think pure thoughts! What a mighty power we can be! United, we can bring forth a spiritual awakening to our communities, our nation, and to the entire world!

Behold, I am coming soon! My reward is with me, and I will give to everyone according to what he has done (Rev. 22:12).

People you know need the opportunity to read this book. You hold in your hands the means of helping many people escape the "carefully devised ambush" of the enemy.

Postlude

Mary and I have read every page in this book many times. Each reading has increased our own joy. We encourage you to re-read each page.

If this book has been a blessing to you, please let us know. Every month we prepare *Praise News* in which we share new things that we learn about praise. We will be pleased to send this to you at no charge, on request. You can contact us at:

Foundation of Praise
PO Box 2518, Dept. B20
Escondido, CA 92033-2518

Or visit us at www.merlincarothers.com

You will also want to read these other best-sellers by Merlin R. Carothers

PRISON TO PRAISE **$3.95**
Many people list this as the most unusual book they have ever read.Millions say it changed their lives and introduced them to the solution to their problems. This is not a book about a prison with bars, but about a prison of circumstances--and how to be set free!

POWER IN PRAISE **$6.95**
Three Million National Bestseller. A simple, clear explanation of how and why the principles introduced in *Prison to Praise* work in every day life.

ANSWERS TO PRAISE **$6.95**
Overjoyed Christians felt compelled to share with Merlin the "signs and wonders" they experienced while practicing the teachings in his first two books.

PRAISE WORKS! **$6.95**
More letters from an assortment of thousands illustrate the secret of *freedom through praise*.

WALKING AND LEAPING **$6.95**
When Merlin and his family rolled over a hill in their new car and trailer they praised the Lord and miracles happened!

BRINGING HEAVEN INTO HELL **$6.95**
Merlin shares new discoveries of how the Holy Spirit sheds light from heaven in the midst of a personal hell.

VICTORY ON PRAISE MOUNTAIN **$6.95**
Spontaneous praise often leads into valleys that are direct paths to higher ground.

THE BIBLE ON PRAISE **$3.75**
A beautiful front cover painting by Merlin featuring his
favorite selected verses on praise from the Bible.

MORE POWER TO YOU **$6.95**
Written for persons in every day places who need more
power in their every day lives.

WHAT'S ON YOUR MIND? **$6.95**
Would you be ashamed for everyone you know to see
your thoughts? If so, you urgently need to read and
understand *What's On Your Mind?*.

LET ME ENTERTAIN YOU **$6.95**
After years of serving the Lord Merlin was eager to
retire. He wanted to rest, relax and enjoy a quiet life,
but God had other plans for him.

FROM FEAR TO FAITH, Revised **$8.95**
God wants to be intimately involved in your life and help
you have victory over your problems? (Read an excerpt at
the end of this book).

YOU CAN BE HAPPY NOW **$8.95**
Everyone desires to be happy! This book will help you to
understand how much God wants you to be happy.

PRAISE CLASSICS **$9.95**
Prison to Praise and *Power in Praise* in a beautiful
hardcover edition.

AWARD WINNING MOVIE

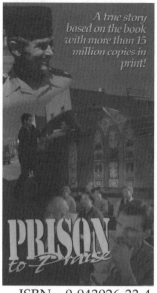

A First Place award
by "National Religious
Broadcasters."

An Angel Award by
"Excellence in Media."

A First Place Covenant
Award by "The Southern
Baptist Radio and
Television Commission."

ISBN   0-943026-33-4

If you didn't believe in miracles before, you will after
watching *Prison to Praise*.

A sixty minute video that will be enjoyed by both
children and adults.

Available for $12.95 from:
Foundation of Praise
PO Box 2518 Dept. M-B20
Escondido CA 92033-2518

An excerpt from Merlin's book *From Fear to Faith*.

The Specter of Fear

Fear lurks in the silent darkness, unwanted – hated. It's power is so great that even when ignored or denied it can still control our destiny.

My first parachute jump was a lesson in sheer terror. The Airborne instructors had vigorously indoctrinated me to believe that I was a tough paratrooper, impervious to fear. Yet I was still afraid.

Ralph Waldo Emerson wrote, "Do the thing you fear and the death of fear is certain." This adage is often true, but I was afraid during my second jump too. I didn't know it then, but my hard lessons in living and coping with the more insidious aspects of fear had just begun. I still had much to learn about fear's enormous capacity to influence our behavior.

We arrived at Fort Benning, Georgia in 1943, two hundred robust, cocky young men from all over the United States. The rigors of infantry basic training were behind us; now we were ready to confront a new challenge – Airborne training.

The grueling physical training we had endured prior to coming to Jump School had, we thought, separated the men from the boys. We were the elite of the Army, we boasted. We could do anything! We eagerly awaited our chance to show the Army what real men were.

Were we afraid? No way! We were embarking on a new and exciting adventure.

The sergeants who greeted us at the bus terminal were seasoned Airborne veterans. They had once been greenhorns like us. They knew our attitudes. The process of ego pulverization was fierce and immediate as they rushed upon us like voracious sharks attacking minnows:

"Pick up those bags, you chicken-livered mama's boys, and let's go!"

Mama's boys? Sergeant, you don't know who you're talking to. We aren't afraid of you or anyone else!

How wrong we were. The sergeants had one primary objective — to separate the men from the boys. In their less-than-humble opinion, the men were those who would never give up despite of injury, suffering – even torture.

In infantry basic training we had learned to run, or so we thought. But at Airborne School we never just went for a run. All we ever did was run, run, and run some more. Anytime we moved it was on the run. We ran to the latrine. We ran to chow. We ran to training sites – five, ten, or more miles. Finally we reached such a high level of fitness that we could run for hours on end without tiring. Failing meant, heaven forbid, washing out of the glorious Airborne.

But running was fun compared with the rigors at the training sites. At one site we were suspended from harnesses like those that would connect us to a parachute from which we would descend from plane to ground. The harness straps, holding our dead weight and digging into our groins, felt like thin wires straining under two hundred pounds of agonized flesh.

About the Author

Merlin R. Carothers' books have been translated into 53 languages. A Master Parachutist in the 82nd Airborne Division during three major campaigns of World War II where he served as a guard to Gen. Dwight D. Eisenhower. Later, as a Lt. Colonel in the U.S. Army Chaplaincy he served in Europe, Korea, the Dominican Republic, Panama and Vietnam. He is a pilot, lecturer and retired pastor. He has made many appearances on national television and has traveled worldwide to share what he has learned about praise.

Merlin and his wife, Mary, live in San Marcos, California.